FOUR QUARTETS –
T S ELIOT AND SPIRITUALITY

FOUR QUARTETS –
T S ELIOT AND
SPIRITUALITY

RICHARD BROCK

PATRICIAN PRESS

MANNINGTREE

Richard Brock is a teacher with degrees in Religious Studies and Mysticism. He has led Religious Studies departments in three UK secondary schools over the last 15 years. He is widely travelled and pursues an interest in life casting during his spare time.

Richard has been studying T. S. Eliot's *Four Quartets* and its influences for 20 years. *Four Quartets – T S Eliot and Spirituality* is his first book. He lives in North-East Essex with his two sons, Noah and Barnaby, and their dog, Sam.

Published by Patrician Press in association with
Richard Brock 2015

First published by Patrician Press in association with Richard Brock 2015

British Library Cataloguing in Publication Data. A catalogue record for this book is available from the British Library.

ISBN 978-0-9932388-0-2 paperback edition

www.patricianpress.com

For Noah and Barnaby

'Se tu segui tua stella, non puoi fallire al glorioso porto, se
ben m'accorsi nella vita bella.'

'If you follow your star, you cannot fail to find your
glorious port, if I discerned rightly in the fair life.'

Dante, Inferno XV:55

CONTENTS

AUTHOR NOTE

T. S. Eliot once remarked that:

'Genuine poetry can communicate before it is understood.'

If you have not read *Four Quartets* before I would suggest an initial reading to experience the language, imagery and music of the poem as communicated by Eliot, without coming to it with any preconceived ideas. Once read – and to those who have already dabbled, a reading of *Four Quartets – T S Eliot and Spirituality* will hopefully be informative, engaging and make you want to hurry back to Eliot for more.

This book is not intended to be a line by line commentary on Eliot's poem. Rather, it is constructed around themes which draw out the essence of the poem. Lines from various movements of *Four Quartets* are woven into my own writing to support and elucidate the themes under discussion. At other times, quotations from *Four Quartets* are isolated and commented upon. In some cases I have had to incorporate Eliot's verses into my text using forward slashes to indicate the beginning and ending of lines, simply because the lines themselves are too long to fit within the width of this book, if isolated. Wherever I have quoted Eliot I have done so in *'italics with inverted commas.'* Whilst the four themes, around which the chapters are based, are specific to *Four Quartets* they are also themes general to spirituality; and, as such, sources other than Eliot and *Four Quartets* are referred to in this book.

RB

April 2015

INTRODUCTION

Thomas Stearns Eliot (1888-1965) was a publisher, playwright, literary critic and one of the twentieth century's major poets. He was born in St. Louis, Missouri, but settled to England in 1914, working and marrying there.

T. S. Eliot first attracted attention for his poem *The Love Song of J. Alfred Prufrock* (1915) which was followed by some of the best-known poems in the English language, including *The Waste Land* (1922) and *Ash Wednesday* (1930). In 1948 he was awarded the Nobel Prize in Literature.

Four Quartets is a set of four poems that were published individually between the years 1935-43. It was Eliot's last major poem.

Burnt Norton is a country house in Gloucestershire, which Eliot visited with his friend Emily Hale in 1934.

East Coker is a Somerset village, near Yeovil. Its church is the final resting place of Eliot, whose ancestors came from the village.

The Dry Salvages are a small group of rocks off the coast of Cape Ann, Massachusetts, USA, located near to the Eliot family's summer retreat and where the young Eliot learnt to sail.

Little Gidding is a hamlet located in Huntingdonshire, which Eliot visited in 1934. It was the home of an Anglican religious community established in 1626 by Nicholas Ferrar. Charles I visited Little Gidding three times.

PREFACE

This short book is written as an introduction to both *Four Quartets* and spirituality. It is an attempt to bring Eliot's poem down from its elevated place on the book shelves of scholars and literary critics and to place it into the hands of those who may not yet have had an opportunity to enjoy this enriching poem; or are perhaps a little intimidated by it.

Much has changed of course, since Eliot's day. The scientific and political advances of the current age provide us with luxuries beyond that of any previous generation – for example, healthcare and hygiene; travel and tourism; technologies which keep us entertained and stimulated; an ever growing media which keeps us both informed and socially connected; and human rights which have ushered in an era of equality for groups previously ostracised, to name but a few.

Religious faith has not fared so well under the growth of these changes. Both the popularity and perception of religion are at an all-time low. A comparison of the UK 2001 and 2011 census reports highlight a decrease in people identifying themselves as Christian by 13%, (to 59% of the population); an increase of people identifying themselves as non-religious by 10%, (to 25% of the population) and a decrease in regular church attendance by 5% (to 6% of the population). It's a pretty sharp decline for 10 years. A recent poll in the Guardian newspaper even reported that 82% of people believed religion does more harm than good.

Commenting on popular perceptions of religion in his own day, the philosopher John Dewey (d.1952) argued that people were losing their religious faith; and not just because the scientific and political advances had provided a more rational alternative, but because they were repelled by the moralising dimension of religion, as well as its historic baggage. For Dewey, 'religion' – as a body or system of beliefs, was actually suppressing or denying the 'religious qualities' that it sought to foster in people; in other words, it was precisely because of religion that many people were no longer even aware of their own spiritual lives. This for Dewey and his followers, was a real concern because, as Abraham Maslow (d.1970) would later put it, 'psychologically, bad things can happen to us if we neglect our spiritual life.'

With the steady decline of the importance and place of these religious or spiritual qualities in a person's life it is perhaps not surprising that at the beginning of the 21st century the individual's sense of security, well-being and overall happiness have become increasingly more dependent on what one might call the finite centres of value and power; that is, material gain, personal appearance and social standing. Not to say there is anything intrinsically wrong with pursuing these things, for they can empower us – but when we rely on them exclusively to provide us with our happiness then we can be left in a potentially vulnerable position. Finite, after all, means perishable and changeable.

So how can people nourish and develop their spiritual lives in a world which is so often measured by material success? Is religion really as barren and inaccessible as many would make it out to be? This book, which has come about as a response to a 20-year study of both spirituality and *Four Quartets*, will explore these questions by examining the spiritual themes underpinning *Four Quartets*. During the years of my studies, as both a student and a teacher, I often found myself looking through the lens of *Four Quartets* in order to understand spirituality as well as, at the same time, looking through the lens of spirituality in order to understand *Four Quartets*. I have adopted this approach in the writing of this book.

The following chapters will discuss four spiritual themes which, being of particular interest to Eliot, underpin *Four Quartets*: Experience, Symbolism, Suffering and Freedom. Each of these themes appears across *Four Quartets* and are not linked with any one Quartet specifically.

Eliot once argued that Dante and Shakespeare divide the modern world between them. In 2015, on the 50th anniversary of Eliot's death, many will revere him not only as the most important poet of the last century but perhaps also as a poet who ranks alongside the greatest in the history of Western literature.

CHAPTER 1:
EXPERIENCE

'To live in eternity and in time is to more widely absorb the one.'
Marsilio Ficino (1433-1499)

The Renaissance philosopher, Marsilio Ficino – following the tradition of the Greek philosopher Plato, wrote that *'the human soul sits on a horizon between Eternity and Time, and is nourished by both these natures.'*

I'm often reminded of Ficino's image when I walk my dog along the seafront where I live. Poised midway on a Rothko canvas is the lighthouse, its lantern tower making a study of the skies whilst its legs stand fixed into the earth – the meeting point of two worlds. Of course, what Ficino was essentially saying is that humans have two centres of value and power. One is to do with the material or physical world the other the spiritual or non-physical.

To speak of centres of value and power is to make reference to those things in our lives which are both important to us (values) and which give us our sense of self-worth and confidence (power). In both we place a certain amount of trust and loyalty; that is, we have faith that they will provide us with our sense of well-being and overall happiness. It follows then that these centres of value and power are also our ultimate concern.

The material centre of value and power is that

which sustains us from a physical perspective and is experienced through our sense perception. The spiritual, likewise sustains us from the non-physical and operates in the realm of abstract ideas and feelings. The two are connected and are woven together to form the complete human experience. When we look at a place of natural beauty, we do so with both our material and spiritual natures – on one level we have a physical encounter with the natural landscape whilst on the other we become are aware of this encounter as 'beautiful' due to the idea or feeling which arises within us and to which we give the name 'beauty'.

Our material nature is sourced from the everyday world around us; from basic needs such as food, shelter and warmth to those of employment, social positioning and financial security. These things are 'valuable' to us because we rely on them in part for our well-being and happiness. A warm home with a fridge full of food and a car on the drive – which are the results of our hard labour and its monetary rewards, afford us a certain level of contentment. Because these material values are finite; that is, they are temporal and impermanent, they are often referred to as belonging to our experience of 'Time.'

In contrast, to use the word spiritual to define a

quality of experience is to call upon such concepts as joy and wonder; beauty and goodness; compassion and humility. We exercise these qualities or 'spiritual values' in our attitudes and actions. For instance, by demonstrating compassion toward someone whose behaviour challenges us or by being lost in wonder at the workings of an ant colony. These spiritual or non-physical values arise from a source which transcends – is located beyond – our everyday concrete physical experience. Humanistic psychology might argue that the source of these values rests in the innate human potential for goodness whilst other psychologies and most philosophies and religions know this source as the ultimate ground of existence, the absolute; the sacred; the divine – or simply God. In this book we shall be referring to this experience as the experience of the 'Timeless.'

Spirituality then is a process of personal transformation through which a person seeks to integrate both of the above values into their life. To balance the material alongside the spiritual and vice versa is to harmonise the two and make them one – much like a pair of binoculars. When the two eye lenses are aligned and become one we get a much clearer perception; when they're not, things appear distorted or blurred and we struggle to see things as they really are.

Spirituality in *Four Quartets* is best understood as a journey through Time to the Timeless; which results in the reconciliation or union of both. It begins with an awakening or what Eliot calls the '*sudden illumination*'. This leads to an awareness of one's over bearing reliance on the material centres of values and power. The poet reflects on:

'*The years of living among the breakage*
Of what was believed in as the most reliable'

Here, the once Time-orientated mind realises that its exclusive pursuit of the finite has been its '*enchainment,*' which '*woven into the weakness of the changing body*' distracts mankind from the reality of the Timeless. '*Caught in the form of limitation,*' this Timeless goes unnoticed by the '*worshippers of the machine.*' But alas, it has been '*waiting, watching and waiting.*'

All journeys involve a departure; and this one begins with the recognition that Time is both the source of human suffering and its potential salvation: '*Only through time is time conquered.*' But, Eliot goes on to tell us: Time itself '*is no healer.*' The '*reconciliation of the timeless with time*' is found to be achieved only through a cleansing – a difficult purging of Time, an emptying of a person's previously held attachments and convictions – which caused him or her to *cling to that dimension.*'

In this purging or *'refining'*, the illumination and awareness of the Timeless becomes stronger. The increased presence of the spiritual leads to an examination of *'all that you have been and done.'* In this there is salvation as one begins to assimilate the *'timeless moments'* into his or her life and is transformed by them. Ultimately, however, these moments can only be sustained properly by a *'lifetime's death in love, ardour and selflessness and self-surrender.'* Hence, the full immersion or *'intersection of the timeless with time'* is not for everyone, but rather is *'an occupation of the saint.'* *'For most of us, this is the aim never here to be realised.'* Instead, our purpose is with the moments *'...in and out of time.'* Moments which temporally raise our consciousness and elevate us to a point on Ficino's horizon where we sit midway between the Timeless and Time to find ourselves nourished by both these natures.

In 1934 T. S. Eliot visited a disused 17th century country house called Burnt Norton on the edge of the Cotswolds in Gloucestershire. The house was in a quiet and remote spot with a view of the Vale of Evesham. Walking into the solitude of the gardens '*in the autumn heat, through the vibrant air,*' Eliot recalls one of these moments of '*sudden illumination.*' Opening a gate leading to a rose garden he stood above a deep, waterless pool. There seemed to be an invisible presence here – '*other echoes*' inhabiting the garden. Even the roses '*Had the look of flowers that are looked at.*' The pool, which was at one moment empty, was then:

'*...filled with water out of sunlight.*'

Eliot, transfixed by the vision goes on:

'*And the lotos rose quietly, quietly.*
The surface glittered out of heart of light'

Then a cloud passed emptying the pool of sunlight. The imagined sound of excited children, hidden in the bushes '*containing laughter*', is broken off by the voice of a bird calling:

'*Go go go said the bird: human kind*
Cannot bear very much reality.
Time past and time future
What might have been and what has been
Point to one end, which is always present.'

The experience Eliot recalls here is often referred to as a 'mystical experience.' In such experiences there is a temporary suspension of the ordinary levels of conscious perception, as an extra-ordinary one breaks through. For Eliot, this breaking through of consciousness is symbolised in the *'shaft of sunlight'* which pours into the dry empty pool – a probable reference to spiritual impoverishment. The lotus flower – an agreed symbol of spirituality, further indicates the presence of the Timeless in this experience.

DRY POOLS IN BURNT NORTON, GLOUCESTERSHIRE

Eliot's reference to the lotus flower is fitting, of course. In Eastern religion the flower symbolises the connection between Time to the Timeless. The plant begins life in the mud (Time) and journeys through the water to the surface into sunlight, where is unfolds its petals and flowers (Timeless). The point is that both Time and the Timeless are necessary conditions for the plant to exist. Whilst it is bathed in the sunlight, it is also rooted in the soil, and vice versa.

In 1917 the German theologian, Rudolf Otto discussed the nature of the mystical experience in his influential book *The Idea of the Holy*. In this work he created the word *'numinous'* (from the Latin 'numen' or spirit) to describe the human encounter with the spiritual. For Otto, the numinous lay beyond our normal sensory perception or rational thought processes and is, therefore, as such *'wholly other.'* He further coined, and made famous, a Latin phrase *mysterium, tremendum et fascinans* to refer to the characteristics of this experience. 'Mysterious' precisely because rational thought alone can neither grasp nor explain the experience; 'tremendous' because it often leaves the individual awestruck and is potentially life changing; and finally 'fascinating' because of the feelings of wonder and longing which accompany it.

The *mysterium, tremendum et fascinans* are found

throughout *Four Quartets.* The following lines in particular capture the otherness, power and enticement of this experience: '*With the drawing of this Love and the voice of this Calling / We shall not cease from exploration.*'

Whilst Otto succeeded in describing the outward characteristics of the mystical experience, explaining something which is beyond the rational workings of the mind is another thing altogether. However, that hasn't stopped a few trying.

In his work, *Religions, Values and Peak Experiences* (1970), the psychologist, Abraham Maslow, took a more scientific approach to mystical experiences. He agreed with John Dewey's assessment of 'religion' and the 'religious' and suggested that religion was actually the enemy of the religious, because it encouraged people to unwittingly suppress their own subjective experiences and replace them with habits and dogmas. For Maslow, the personal or subjective 'religious' experience was at the core of every religion and every religious revelation.

'*The very beginning, the intrinsic core, the essence, the universal nucleus of every known high religion has been the private, lonely, personal illumination, revelation or ecstasy of some acutely sensitive prophet or seer.*'

Maslow called these mystical experiences 'peak experiences' and, having collected and examined reports of these experiences, argued that a peak experience is a perfectly natural human phenomena which can be examined today. He did not consider ancient reports of peak experiences (which, he reminds us, are phrased in the mythic and linguistic context of that age and culture) to be particularly unique either – since everyone has either had or is capable of having a peak experience. It is important to note here, however, that Maslow wasn't denying the existence of a Timeless reality – rather, he was attempting to reclaim the 'religious' from the monopoly of 'religion.' (As mentioned earlier, Maslow believed spirituality was essential for psychological well-being). He described peak experiences as:

'Rare, exciting, oceanic, deeply moving, exhilarating, elevating experiences that generate an advanced form of perceiving reality, and are even mystic...'

Most people are familiar with Maslow's pyramid shaped hierarchy of needs – the stages of development which Maslow thought a person passes through during their life. The five tiers begin with 'physiological' and move through 'safety', 'love', 'self-esteem' and finally the 'growth needs' or so called 'self-actualisation.' According to Maslow, a person must satisfy the lower level basic needs before progressing on to meet the higher level growth needs. Like Ficino, Maslow thought the human condition had, as he put it, *'a two-fold nature.'* His hierarchy of needs reflect this value system. The first four needs sit within what he termed the 'D Values' (or 'deficiency' cognition). Maslow referred to these as the *'the normal, natural, human and every day.'* These values correspond well with Eliot's experience of Time in *Four Quartets*. The last, the growth needs, he placed within the B Values (or 'being' cognition). These are a person's spiritual needs, which include the need for truth, beauty and goodness, as well as unity. These values are comparable to Eliot's experience of the Timeless in *Four Quartets*. Importantly, Maslow thought self-actualisation and B Values, were actually facilitated through peak experiences. Like Eliot's *'Intersection of the timeless with time'*, Maslow spoke of the unitive life as the ability to:

'...perceive both the sacred and profane aspects of a person: Not perceiving both the universal, eternal, infinite,

essential symbolic qualities is certainly a kind of reduction to the concrete.

'In my own phrasing, this is the fusion of the Being realm and the Deficiency realm; to be aware of the B realm while immersed in the D realm. This is nothing new. Any reader of mystical literature knows what I'm talking about.'

We can find fairly contemporary examples of Maslow's peak experiences through the media of film. Indeed, Rudolf Otto – referring to the numinous in *The Idea of the Holy,* remarked that films *'fill a need in us'* since they *'...articulate our thoughts and feelings in a metaphorical and symbolic way.'* One film which articulates such an experience is the 1999 Oscar winning film *American Beauty*. In this film we meet the character Ricky Fitts, an eighteen-year-old loner who spends much of his time recording trivial events on his camcorder. One of these events, in particular, captures something of what Eliot records in his poetry in the gardens of *Burnt Norton*. Sitting in his bedroom, Ricky shows his girlfriend, Jane, the most beautiful thing he has ever filmed: It is a plastic bag being carried in circles by the wind. One moment it is lifted violently skywards and the next moment it floats gracefully back to the ground;

before being lifted up again. As they watch the film, Ricky discusses these moments:

> *'It was one of those days when it's a minute away from snowing. And there's this electricity in the air, you can almost hear it, right? And this bag was just (he pauses) dancing with me. Like a little kid begging me to play with it. For fifteen minutes. That's the day I realised that there is this entire life behind things, and this incredibly benevolent force that wants me to know there is no reason to be afraid, ever. Video's a poor excuse, I know. But it helps me remember. I need to remember. Sometimes there's so much beauty in the world I feel I can't take it and that my heart is going to cave in.'*

Ricky offers us a modern day model of a peak experience which draws obvious parallels with Eliot's experience in *Four Quartets*. Compare the atmospheres – which Ricky describes as '*electricity*' and Eliot recalls as '*autumn heat*' and '*vibrant air*.' Ricky speaks of the presence of a '*benevolent force*' that wanted him to know that all was well, whereas Eliot talks of '*other echoes*' inhabiting the garden and the sense of joy, experienced as '*heart of light*.' Later in the poem, Eliot begins to conclude his experience with the line '*All shall be well and all manner of thing shall be well*.'

Ricky talks of the need to remember; and this too is an important element of Eliot's experience of the Timeless. In *Burnt Norton* he entices us to follow him into the garden with '*Footfalls*' which '*echo in the memory.*' Later he speaks of us having '*had the experience but missed the meaning*' and that '*approach to the meaning restores the experience*' for this, ultimately, '*is the use of memory – for liberation.*'

In the above I have talked fairly extensively of Abraham Maslow's humanistic theories of religion and offered a contemporary example of a peak experience via the film, *American Beauty*. I feel this is important for our understanding of both *Four Quartets* and spirituality as these works draw out difficult concepts within alternative contexts – which might be a useful entry point for those new to the study of spirituality.

Returning to *Four Quartets* and the gardens of the Gloucestershire country house, where we are both in Time and out of Time – Eliot has opened the '*first gate*' which leads us into a rose garden; but he is also, we are informed, leading us into our '*first world.*' Here, we are transported to the Garden of Eden – symbolic landscape and home of the Timeless and eternal; the place of the original temptation and man's consequent fall from grace. Eliot brings us back to this place time and again throughout the whole poem to remind us of our spiritual heritage; as in, for example *East Coker*:

> *'Whisper of running streams and winter lightening*
> *The Wild Thyme unseen and the wild strawberry*
> *The laughter in the garden, echoed ecstasy.'*

Eliot goes on to tell us that this is *'Not lost, but requiring'*, that is; we can get back to this symbolic state. This is, as Eliot puts it, our true *'Calling.'* And so:

> *'We shall not cease from exploration*
> *And the end will be to arrive at where we first started*
> *And know the place for the first time*
> *Through the unknown remembered gate'*

The experience in the garden of *Burnt Norton* offered *'Hints and guesses'* of what Ricky Fitts called *'the entire life behind things.'* It may be only a *'little consciousness'* that Time allows but these experiences whet the appetite for the greater reality that is the Timeless. The task then is one of reconciliation – to *'recover what has been lost'* and to become the meeting point of these two worlds. It is perhaps interesting to note, in reference to this reconciliation, that the word 'religion,' which originates from the Latin verb '*religare*' means '*to bind back.*' This is encountered also in the Eastern traditions, where the word '*yoga*' which corresponds to our word 'religion' itself also means to '*yoke*' or '*to bind.*' It is the binding back or yoking of these two dimensions of experience – Time and the Timeless. This is the function of religion. At the beginning of the poem Eliot says Time is 'unredeemable' that is; Time *alone* cannot redeem (the word redeem from the Latin verb '*reimere*' means to '*take back*'). Time cannot take us back to our natural condition, to a symbolic Eden. This can only be achieved when, as Maslow states, the material is fused with the spiritual.

This theme of a '*requiring*' or necessary reconciliation of the Timeless with Time is expressed elsewhere in *Four Quartets* in the concept of the still point. Here, Eliot takes us beyond the shafts of sunlight – the experience of the '*timeless moment*' in the rose garden at *Burnt Norton*; and beyond even the symbolic recollections of Eden, to the very beginning of Time and creation: '*At the Still point of the turning world. / Neither flesh nor fleshless; / Neither from nor towards; at the still point, there the dance is...*'

It is here, at the '*still point*', that all the multiplicity and clutter, '*the dance*' of Time is ordered; and everything with it too – be it, as the second movement of *Burnt Norton* puts it: '*garlic and sapphires*' or '*boarhound and boar.*' All is '*reconciled among the stars.*'

To understand where Eliot is taking us with this '*still point*' we need – and not for the last time – to refer to the work of the individual who Eliot spoke of as the one who '*made the spiritual visible*' – the 13th century author of the *Divine Comedy*, Dante Alighieri. We will speak of Dante himself in more depth in our later chapter on suffering. But, for the moment, we need to pass on Dante himself in order to briefly explore his cosmology.

It was the Greek philosopher Aristotle (d.322 BCE) who first advanced the idea of an 'unmoved mover' – a self-existent being located in an outer void beyond the sphere of the fixed stars. Dante developed this idea into a cosmology in which all creation, including, what the ancients called, the primum mobile (the outer universe), the fixed stars, the planets and the Earth are set in motion from a single unmoved point existing in the empyrean, which is a motionless point of pure light beyond the primum mobile.

Referring to the empyrean, *Four Quartets* comments:

'The light is still at the still point of the turning world'.

In the third book of the *Divine Comedy*, *Paradise* – Dante's heavenly guide Beatrice speaks of this still point when she says:

'From that one point hang all the heavens and all of nature.'

For Dante, the Timeless 'unmoved mover,' is love – the source from which all things emanate. The last lines of *Paradise* comment:

'Like a wheel that spins with even motion revolved by the Love that moves the sun and the other stars.'

Likewise, Eliot, who in the closing movement of *Burnt Norton*, comments:

'Love itself is unmoving,
Only the cause and end of all movement
Timeless...'

The primum mobile is where Time began. In canto XXVII of *Paradise*, Dante tells us that Time is like a tree – the roots are in the Timeless and Time appears as the leaves.

Compare to the second movement in *Burnt Norton*:

'*We move above the moving tree*
In light upon the figured leaf'

Time and the motion of all things is the passage through which the love of God passes from the realm of the Timeless into the realm of the temporal. The Primum Mobile is therefore the bridge between the material world and the spiritual. For Dante, it was the source of all things created and uncreated. Eliot shares this view – again, using the word '*dance*' in place of creation or Time:

> '*Except for the point, the still point,*
> *There would be no dance.*'

In *Four Quartets* the very essence of our lives originates in the still point too. In the second movement we find reference to the '*trilling wire*' in our blood which '*dances*' through our arteries and circulates, all of which are '*figured in the drift of stars*' (grows out of the roots of the Timeless). Eliot further comments: '*I can only say, there we have been: but I cannot say where. / And I cannot say how long, for that is to place it in time.*'

Of course, in the 13th century the solar system was thought to be geocentric, with the Earth taking centre stage and the heavenly bodies including the sun revolving around it. This changed in the 16th century when Copernicus and others risked persecution by daring to suggesting a sun-centred solar system by way of a heliocentric model. So, does it matter that we now know Dante's version of the solar system does not exist, and that there is no such thing as the primum mobile? Does it render all of this cosmology as nonsense? As we shall see in the next chapter, religious language is largely poetic and mythic. It is a world constructed out of metaphor and symbol. And it is no different here where Dante constructs images which reflect something of our interior lives and which help facilitate an understanding of the relationship between God, the Timeless and creation, Time. The Timeless both transcends creation and is immanent in creation. This essence exists prior to our existence and our life and all life is contingent upon it. Just how are you going to go about expressing that meaningfully without some imagination?

In exploring this theme of reconciliation we should also discuss the epigraphs (quotations) which Eliot gives us before his poem begins. There are two, both relevant to our current theme and both from the Greek philosopher, Heraclitus (d.475 BCE). The first states that:

> 'Although the logos is common to all, many people lived as though they had a wisdom of their own.'

I have deliberately omitted a translation of the word *logos* here since it needs some explanation. First thing to say is that the logos is a sacred word which has many uses and meanings; *'reasoning'* (think of the word *logic* or any *ology* you may have studied – well, it originated here), '*life force*' which pervades the universe (aka '*anima mundi* or soul of the world') and 'Word' which Christians know from the *Gospel of St John* ('In the beginning was the Word'). Hence, Logos is typically identified with Christ. In terms of how Eliot used it in *Four Quartets*, I would say probably all three ways, depending on what part of *Four Quartets* you are reading. Regarding how it relates to our discussion on reconciliation, we need only recall that the '*intersection of the timeless with time*' is understood as nothing other than the alignment of our non-physical (or spiritual) with our physical (or material) natures. For many people however, this understanding or wisdom is either – as Eliot puts it in *Little Gidding*: '*not known, because not looked for*' or perhaps '*...heard, half heard.*' And so, by default it seems, many people live with only a partial wisdom – the one rooted in their temporal experience.

The second of the epigraphs, can again be cleverly applied to different contexts within the *Four Quartets*.

'*The way up and the down are one in the same*'

In the final chapter we will discuss Eliot's spiritual path – the '*via negativa*', or negative way. In this, the 'way down' is a process of detachment from the material, which leads to the 'way up' and a connection to the spiritual. Here, however, in our discussion on reconciliation, we might want to think back to Dante's tree metaphor – where the tree's roots are in the Timeless whilst its leaves flutter in Time. When this unity is realised (i.e. the way up and the way down are the same) then, as our compound ghost in the second movement of *Little Gidding* puts it:

'Two worlds become much like each other'

Moving on to the final part of this chapter, we need to consider how our discussion on the reconciliation of these 'two worlds' of value and power – the Timeless and Time – relates to Christianity.

Although Christianity underpins significant parts of *Four Quartets* thinking, Eliot only ever really appears to make a passing mention of it; and he does as much with Hinduism and Buddhism. Consider the two lines in the fifth movement of *Burnt Norton* – where there is a fleeting though obvious reference to Jesus in: *'The Word in the desert/Is most attacked by voices of temptation.'* In the third movement of *East Coker*, we can infer allusions to Jesus in the lines

'*The wounded surgeon plies the steel which questions the distempered part.*' And a few lines below this, there is the reference to the '*...dying nurse/whose constant care is not to please/But to remind of our and Adam's curse.*' Again, we may interpret a link to the Church. It's not until we get to the end of *Dry Salvages* and onto *Little Gidding* that Christianity is really announced in *Four Quartets*. But before all this, Eliot, sweeps away any pseudo mystical spirituality which might purport a claim to the Timeless.

In the final movement of *Dry Salvages*, Eliot ridicules these supernatural diviners. The communication of aliens and spirits; observations made by astrologers, palmists, tarot readers and dream interpreters; or the use of experimental drugs. All these, he writes, are mere pastimes and '*features of the press*' and apparently always will be: '*Whether on the shores of Asia, or in the Edgware Road. / Men's curiosity searches past and future / And clings to that dimension.*'

Having suitably disregarded these mere curiosities Eliot goes on to tell us that though we may have had visions or peak experiences in shafts of sunlight – our '*moments in and out of time*' – and though we may have had a longing for Eden (a place of peace and sacredness which Eliot evokes in the lines '*the wild thyme unseen*' and '*the waterfall*') '*to apprehend the point of intersection of the timeless with time*', is the aim most of us can never realise. And it may, as the poet has already told us in the final section of *East Coker*, have only ever really happened (been discovered or conquered) just once or twice, '*by men one cannot hope to emulate.*' Here, at the end of *Dry Salvages*, Eliot finally pins his colours to the mast: '*The hint half guessed, the gift half understood, is Incarnation / Here the impossible union / Of spheres of existence is actual, / Here the past and future / Are conquered, and reconciled.*'

The key word here of course is 'Incarnation.' Think – 'chilli con carne' or 'chilli with meat.' Incarnation means 'to go into the flesh.' As a Christian term, which has its equivalent in the East in the word 'avatar,' it is the descent of God into the flesh, the human form. Incarnation in Christianity refers to the embodiment and reconciliation of the Timeless and Time in the person of Jesus of Nazareth, later Jesus Christ.

Jesus then, for Eliot, was the exemplar for mankind; the conqueror of Time – a moment in history when the unimaginable intersection of the Timeless with Time actually took place. Through the gospels, one can encounter this intersection or, as Christians call it, this revelation or 'The Light of the World.' The teachings, the stories, the commentaries and letters of the *New Testament* are each thought to offer a direct line of communication with, and instruction from, this '*impossible union of spheres*.' By the person of Jesus Christ, this union was made flesh and walked upon the earth. The bridge between Time and the Timeless was repaired (having been temporarily weakened by the appearance of sin in the world (Chapter Three deals with the concept of sin).

According to Christianity, it is because of this person, that we are able to walk back through our first gate and into our first world, and return to Eden. In the 17th century, this is precisely what one Christian community in particular did, through their '*observance, thought and action*' making present '*the intersection of the timeless moment*' in England, in a place called Little Gidding.

In the 17th century, Nicholas Ferrah and his family established a Christian community at Little Gidding under strict Christian routine – a member of the family was at prayer in the church, day and night. The community formed a strong relationship with the Christian poet George Herbert and it was a refuge for King Charles after the Battle of Naseby, during the English Civil War. Eliot visited Little Gidding in 1934 and, in *Four Quartets*, revered the sacredness of the place:

'*You are not here to verify,*
Instruct yourself, or inform curiosity
Or carry report. You are here to kneel.'

In this final poem, *Little Gidding* – the hamlet and community – becomes the '*nearest, in place and time*' to have grounded the 'Timeless moment' in a specifically Christian context. We are not, however, in '*time's covenant*' in the poem and this is no pilgrimage to Huntingdonshire; rather, it is an exploration of the experience of intersection, where we are '*suspended in time*' between frost and fire, pole and tropic, melting and freezing. Here, opposites are reconciled and '*two worlds become much like each other.*' Further, in *Little Gidding*, Eliot reflects on the '*rough road*' we will have travelled to arrive at this place and what its ultimate fulfilment might mean.

In this chapter we have discussed our centres of value and power, Eliot's encounter with the Timeless in the gardens of *Burnt Norton* and his allusions to the garden of Eden. We have briefly explored the nature of mystical experience as presented in the influential writings of Rudolf Otto and we have had a whistle stop tour of Maslow's humanistic ideas on religion, peak experiences and values. The film *American Beauty* has provided a modern mystical experience comparable to Eliot's and our discussion on the 'still point' has further elucidated our understanding of the relationship between Time and the Timeless and the required reconciliation of both. Finally, we have begun to consider how these ideas relate to Christianity through the person of Jesus Christ, in whom *'the impossible union of spheres of existence'* was made actual.

Our next theme 'symbolism' has been kicking her heels impatiently, waiting in the corridors outside our discussion. She has been kept long enough, perhaps too long; and we can go no further on this journey without her. Before we do move on however, I leave you with a quotation from the German philosopher and winner of the 1908 Nobel Prize for Literature, Rudolf Eucken (d.1926). Eliot attended classes given by Eucken at both Harvard and in Marburg, Germany, and he aptly concludes our chapter on Experience with the following statement. The task of man, he said, is to:

'...distinguish within himself the narrower and the larger life, the life that is finite and can never transcend itself, and an infinite life through which he enjoys communion with the immensity and truth of the universe. Can man rise to this spiritual level? On the possibility of

his doing so rests all our hope of supplying any meaning or value to life.'

CHAPTER 2:
SYMBOLISM

'It is in and through Symbols that man, consciously or unconsciously, lives, works, and has his being...'
Thomas Carlyle (1795-1181)

'No world view of yesterday, today or tomorrow is definitive.' Thus spoke Rudolph Bultmann, in his seminal work *Jesus and Mythology* (1958). Bultmann was a twentieth century German theologian, who I happened upon in the first year of my undergraduate studies. I was in Hay on Wye with a friend on a five day camping 'retreat', so called. It was actually five days of silence whilst following the Offa's Dike trail through the Black Mountains on the English/ Welsh border. We signed our way when we needed to communicate to one another and held up a left horizontal index finger midway on top of a right vertical one to indicate our requirements for tea, if

and when we came upon a town with a café. It wasn't just silence though; we also had a day of fasting, held a one night vigil in the woods outside our tents (alternating turns to stay awake for two hours at a time) and performed symbolic rituals on the evening fire – I burnt a piece of rope I had found, to symbolise detachment (detaching myself from my senses, some might say). And so it was that, feeling suitably spiritual, I found myself, in the summer of 1995, browsing the shelves marked Religion and Philosophy in one of the many book shops in Hay on Wye. My rucksack was already bulging with the rectangular goods when my fingers rested on the thin red spine of Bultmann's book. It was the last book I bought before heading for the bus back to London. I could overstate its significance to me by suggesting that it was *the* most important book I'd ever bought, *in my life*. But I'll resist the temptation; rather, it was the second.

In *Jesus and Mythology*, Bultmann outlined the differences between the mythological and the scientific conceptions of the world and suggested that it would require a *sacrificum intellectus* on the part of modern man in order to accept a supernatural explanation of the world; one made up of Heaven, Hell, gods and evil spirits. Further, it simply makes no sense to talk of a Son of God, begotten of the Holy Spirit, born of virgin who came into the world to atone with his own blood the sins of all humanity; who died, rose again three days later and then ascended to heaven. Such conceptions of the world are, as Bultmann put it *'over and done with.'*

In response to the issue of the conflict between the scientific and mythological world views, Bultmann called for the *'demythologisation'* of religious teaching. This involves suspending our often literal interpretations of its myths in order to recover the deeper spiritual meaning concealed inside; and to reinterpret it for the modern ear. To this end, Bultmann called for the demythologisation of *The New Testament* to make it more relevant, accessible and ultimately more meaningful for a modern day reader. It was not the first time that a light had been shone on religious language as a potential barrier to a successful understanding of religious teachings – discussions about the differences between the Jesus of history and the Christ of faith had already highlighted this problem and been smouldering in the background for decades, but it was Bultmann's book, *Jesus and Mythology*, which ignited the whole issue; setting a beacon to enable others to navigate their way into the depths of religious teaching.

Demythologising is about unpacking symbols.

Fortunately, we already have the tools to enable us to do this. For instance, take a look back at the previous sentences. I used the metaphor of shining a light and barriers to describe the experience many people face when reading or hearing religious teachings and stories. I then commented on the need to use tools to enable us to unpack myths. These are metaphors or symbols; and we use them every day to create images which enable us to make sense of our experiences and to share them with others. We do it with our language and of course, we do it with our body. I just now waved my hand at a neighbour passing my house. It's a hand, it's at the end of my wrist. I held it up and motioned it left to right. The action itself is meaningless unless the symbolism behind the action is understood. I think I may have confused my neighbour, had I stood on one leg and with the other waved my foot! I would be communicating nothing in this action other than perhaps that I am having an off day. Our well-exercised use of metaphors and symbols in our everyday lives will help us understand religion, precisely because it is through metaphors and symbols that religious ideas express themselves.

If I say to you that '*I'm all ears*' you don't expect to see me suddenly covered, head to toe, in ears. You immediately understand that this is a metaphor for *'I'm listening.'* This is because you know, or have a 'heads up' (more metaphors!) on the context in which I am applying the term – *'I'm all ears.'* The philosopher Ludwig Wittgenstein (d.1951) argued that the meaning of words is in their use; that is, the function they perform as agreed by a particular group or society. He called these 'language games.' We have already highlighted the difficulty we have in assimilating the world view and language of a people who thought mythologically with those who think scientifically; and this is where the issue with demythologising gets tricky. We have the tools to unpack the myths, but what is the new context in which we are going to be able to understand the deeper spiritual meaning revealed inside the myth?

For Bultmann, that context was existentialism – the philosophy which promotes awareness of the essential freedom and responsibility that comes with living a truly authentic human existence. And for Bultmann, Christ was the model of that authenticity. Many people have reinterpreted their own religion and this has become their new context – which is the reason why today there are thousands of denominations or versions of Christianity. New religious movements offer alternative contexts, as does Humanism. And there are the many people who prefer simply to call themselves 'spiritual' rather than clothe their spirituality in a particular religious or philosophical context. Whether we stick with the old context, take on a new one or choose no context, spirituality and personal transformation is at the core of all these contexts, old and new.

Spirituality, which Marsilio Ficino said '*is as natural to man as barking is to a dog*', adds depth and meaning to our lives. You will recall from our previous discussion on centres of value and power that spirituality is ultimately, a set of values which, independent of the physical world, have their origins in love and humility; selflessness and self-awareness; appreciation of beauty and wonder (in the ordinary as well as the extraordinary). Spiritual values promote happiness and well-being through experiences which genuinely empower us and others, which are not dependent on the finite or material and which foster a caring approach to the environment in which we live and share. For many, these values have their source in all that is both innate and potential in humans; for others, the source of these values is God.

Spirituality itself is not dependent on any one time period or religion. Both act as vehicles through which spiritual values pass – via the narratives and teachings of the communities which represent these time periods or religions. The early Greek historian, Plutarch (d.120 CE) records that a sailor, on his way to Italy from one of the Greek Islands, once heard a divine voice call out to him from across the sea, instructing him that he was to tell the world that 'the great god Pan is dead.' Christian writer, C. K. Chesterton, said that 'Pan died the night Christ was born.' Here we get a real sense of spirituality passing from one religion – or one era and context, to that of another. The writer, Aldous Huxley, called spirituality 'The Perennial Philosophy' because spirituality transcends time and religion and outlasts them both.

In reading Four Quartets, it is important that we have a developed understanding of how religious language works, precisely because Eliot's own religion is the backdrop to the poem. Negative perceptions people have of religion are often rooted in the ignorance of how religious language operates – which is the reason why, understandably, religion – and regrettably five thousand years of human enquiry, is sometimes brushed aside as 'old hat.'

Demythologising the Christian story then will involve unpacking its myths and symbols and placing these within a spiritual context we can understand. This means seeing these stories purely in terms of what they teach us about personal transformation – love, humility, forgiveness, etc.

You will recall that for Eliot, spirituality reached its fullness in the person of Christ, who for Eliot, represented what he called the '*impossible union of sphere*' (the union of the Timeless in Time – the incarnation).

Understanding something of the spirituality of the Christian message will support us in understanding Eliot, where he makes references to religion, which might otherwise confuse us. For instance, take the line from the fourth movement of *East Coker*:

> '*The dripping blood our only drink,*
> *The bloody flesh our only food*'

Of course, we are not so ignorant as to think that Eliot is here advocating cannibalism. But nevertheless, such verses can alienate if we are not familiar with their context. If this is so, we need to crack open the myth in order to discover the spiritual significance of the Last Supper, where Christ offered his disciples bread and wine, and told them it was his body and blood; and instructed them to eat and drink in remembrance of him. Is this, and Eliot's reference to it, not perhaps a simple teaching about the importance of spiritual values in sustaining us, like food? The story of the feeding of the five thousand and the Lord's Prayer: 'Give us this day, our daily bread' offer a similar wisdom.

And further, the lines from the fourth movement of Little Gidding:

'The dove descending breaks the air
With flame of incandescent terror
Of which the tongues declare
The one discharge of sin and error.'

A dove is on fire, both terrorising and liberating us. What's going on? The reference itself is, in part, the myth of Jesus' baptism by John, in the River Jordan. In this story a dove descends from the sky, followed immediately by a booming voice saying 'This is my son, in whom I am well pleased.' The dove, of course, is the symbol of the spirit, our spiritual life. It represents the Timeless descending into Time, into the person of Jesus of Nazareth who is the incarnation, the fulfilment of this union; he is the khristos, the māshīah – the holy one of God. Break the myth behind Eliot's lines: Love will purge you, cleanse you from selfishness, greed, pride, etc. (The next chapter will discuss the meaning of 'sin' and the seven deadly sins.)

Demythologising the myths of Athens or Christianity is not to say that these world views are completely defunct – of course, for millions of people these stories remain the context which nourishes their spiritual lives, but for many others, the stories alienate them. Simply put, in the form of *nota bene* – take note; when reading religion, you may need to do as Thomas Carlyle famously said, *'empty-out the bathing-tub, but not the baby along with it.'*

A final few thoughts on the topic of demythologisation from the influential Theologian, Paul Tillich (d.1965) who, agreeing with Bultmann, argued that *'breaking the myth'* was sometimes necessary, to *'make conscious its symbolic character.'* Resistance to demythologisation, he argued, gives birth to literalism – which, for Tillich, *'draws God down to the level of the finite and conditional'* in a negative sense.

Tillich further argued that *'Man's ultimate concern must be expressed symbolically, because symbolic language alone is able to express the ultimate.'* It is for this reason that Tillich thought religious language is closer to poetry than prose. In *Four Quartets*, Eliot uses metaphors and symbols extensively, and not just because this is what poets do, but rather because the nature of his subject, spirituality, demands it. Spirituality, of all human endeavours, is the most difficult to express and talk about. To this issue we must now turn.

In *Varieties of Religious Experience* (1902), an important and influential work in the study of mysticism, William James (d.1910), whose classes Eliot attended at Harvard, proposed a criterion by which an experience may be justly called mystical. This is known as the 'four marks of mystic states.' The first of these, relevant to our discussion, is *ineffability*. Of this, James wrote:

> '*The subject of it* [mysticism] *immediately says that it defies expression, that no adequate reports of its content can be given in words.*'

In *Burnt Norton*, Eliot writes of the '*intolerable wrestle with words and meaning.*' Further, he comments on the difficulty of expressing the seemingly inexpressible:

> '*Words strain,*
> *Crack and sometimes break, under the burden*
> *Under the tension, slip, slide, perish,*
> *Will not stay still.*'

William James further states that as a result of ineffability, the mystical experience can only be experienced directly:

[handwritten margin note: incapable of being express in words]

'It follows from this that its quality must be directly experienced; it cannot be imparted or transferred to others.'

Interestingly, the word mysticism, from the verb *mu*, which is Greek in origin, means '*to remain silent.*' Other familiar words derived from *mu* include *mumble*, *mutter*, and *mute*. Those familiar with Zen Buddhism will know that the Japanese term *mu* is a term of negation meaning 'nothing.' Nothing can accurately express the enlightenment experience. Words always fall short. The finite, cannot express the infinite.

Eliot comments on the difficulty of using words to convey mystical experience: '*Trying to use words, and every attempt / Is a wholly new start, and a different kind of failure / Because one has only learnt to get the better of words / For the thing one no longer has to say, or the way in which / One is no longer disposed to say it.*'

It seems that Eliot would need more than a direct approach, if he were to find words to measure up to the ineffable.

In 1908, a twenty-year-old T. S. Eliot came across a book by Arthur Symons entitled: *The Symbolist Movement in Literature.* This book would shape Eliot's poetry throughout his life and in particular give him the tools to enable him to articulate the ineffable, in *Four Quartets*. Eliot refers to the significance of the book:

> 'The kind of poetry that I needed to teach me the use of my own voice did not exist in English at all, it was only to be found in French.
>
> 'Without the tradition which starts with Baudelaire and culminates in Valery, my own work would hardly be conceivable.'

The tradition which Symons had introduced to Eliot was named by critics as the Symbolists movement. It began with Charles Baudelaire and included the French poets Stéphane Mallarmé, Paul Verlaine, Paul Valery and Arthur Rimbaud. The group lived a bohemian lifestyle and met regularly at Mallarmé's well-known 'salons', at his home on the Rue de Rome, Paris. These intellectual gatherings attracted the poets Oscar Wilde, Rainer Maria Rilke, and W. B. Yeats; the painters – Renoir, Monet and Degas, and the sculptor Rodin, among others. Those who attended became known as 'Les Mardistes', 'The Tuesdays' a reference to the day they met.

The characteristics of this poetic movement are an attempt to suggest rather than describe; to evoke feelings, moods or experiences rather than make direct identification or lucid statements. The poetry was intuitive and broke away from traditional conventions of rigid form and structure. Rhythm, rhyme and stanza were loosened and often the arrangement of words and spaces on the page where liberated to encourage a musicality beyond rhyme. *'I do not transgress measure, only disperse it,'* said Mallarmé. His *Un coup de dés jamais n'abolira le hazard* (A throw of the dice will never abolish chance) is perhaps a more extreme example of this.

In *Four Quartets*, Eliot is at the height of his poetic power, as he both suggests and evokes; enticing us and drawing us away from the world of Time, into the solitude of our inner world and the silence of the ineffable Timeless moment.

> *'Footfalls echo in the memory*
> *Down the passage which we did not take*
> *Towards the door we never opened*
> *Into the rose-garden. My words echo*
> *Thus, in your mind.*
> > *But to what purpose*
> *Disturbing the dust on a bowl of rose-leaves*
> *I do not know.*
> > *Other echoes*
> *Inhabit the garden. Shall we follow?'*

In terms of music, the title *Four Quartets* goes

much deeper than the mere comparison between the four sections of the poem and that of a musical quartet. Notice the arrangement of the words, the spacing of the text – the surrounding silence; like the silent beats between notes of music. This is more evident when you read the poem aloud or hear the poem spoken: the musical impact of the language, metres and rhymes crystallises with the meaning and releases the emotion. The appeal to the senses, above that of the cerebral, is another Symbolist trait.

Four Quartets is thought to have been inspired by one of Beethoven's late string quartets – Opus 132 in A minor. In a letter dated 1931, Eliot commented to friend and fellow poet, Stephen Spender that:

'I have the A minor Quartet on the gramophone, and I find it quite inexhaustible to study. There is a sort of heavenly, or at least more than human gaiety, about some of his later things which one imagines might come to oneself as the fruit of reconciliation and relief after immense suffering; I should like to get something of that into verse before I die.'

In the second half of the first movement of *Burnt Norton* the sun for a moment shines through the cloud and the entire deserted garden seems to become alive. Here, there is a change of rhythm and melody as new accompaniments enter the musical landscape:

'Dry the pool, dry concrete, brown edged,
And the pool was filled with water out of sunlight
And the lotos rose, quietly, quietly,
The surface glittered out of heart of light,
And they were behind us, reflected in the pool.
Then a cloud passed, and the pool was empty.'

Shafts of sunlight fill the dry pool of Time as the Timeless descends, much like it will later, in *Little Gidding*, in the form of the dove.

Later, in the fourth movement of *Burnt Norton*, there is a shift to more sombre tones creating a darker atmosphere; a dulling of the senses, as the Timeless moment withdraws:

'Time and the bell have buried the day,
The black cloud carries the sun away'

The Symbolist believed that the purpose of art was not merely to represent reality but to access greater truths, through symbols. Symons wrote that the symbolist movement was itself an attempt to 'spiritualise literature'

'In a Symbol, there is ever, more or less distinctly and directly, some embodiment and revelation of the infinite; the infinite is made to blend itself with the finite, to stand visible, and as it were, attainable there.'

Symons further commented in *The Symbolist Movement in Literature*, that:

'With a change of men's thought comes a change of literature. After the world has starved its soul long enough in the contemplation and the rearrangement of material things, there comes the turn of the soul; and with it a literature in which the visible world is no longer a reality, and the unseen world no longer a dream.'

There are echoes of the Symbolists elsewhere in *Four Quartets*. Eliot makes several direct references to Mallarmé, for example:

'Since our concern was speech, and speech impelled us
To purify the dialect of the tribe'

The above lines echo those of Mallarmé in his poem *Le Tombeau Edgar Poe*, where he suggests it is a poet's job to:

'Donner un sens plus pur aux mots de la tribu'

(*'give a purer sense to the words of the tribe'*)

The famous literary critic F.R. Leavis suggested that Eliot was *'recalling Mallarmé'* in the *Burnt Norton* line:

'*And the unseen eyebeam crossed, for the roses*
Had the look of flowers that are looked at.'

Compare to Mallarmé's poem, Brise Marine (Sea Breeze):

'*Rien, ni les vieux jardins reflétés par les yeux. Ne retiendra ce Coeur*'

('*Nothing, not old gardens reflected in the eyes. Will retain this Heart*')

Eliot acknowledges Mallarmé's influence on him elsewhere in the difficult verses of the second movement of *Burnt Norton*:

'*Garlic and Sapphires in the mud*
Clot the bedded axle-tree.'

We have discussed the relevance of these lines in

our previous chapter, but note here the immediate impact these two polar opposite subjects have on the senses, a very symbolist approach: garlic – dull, earthy and time-bound and sapphires – dazzling, desired and sublime.

Compare to the sections of a sonnet by Mallarmé:

'*Tonnerre et rubis aux moyeux*'
('*Thunder and rubies in the axles*')

No doubt, combined in Eliot's mind with Mallarmé's poem, *Le Tomebeau de Charles Baudelaire*:

'*Bavant boue et rubis*'
('*Slobber of mud and rubies*')

In the fifth movement of *East Coker*, Eliot refers to the use of words to capture the Timeless as '*a raid on the inarticulate.*' In this chapter we have seen that Eliot's use of metaphors and symbols, coupled with our own understanding of how religious language works, can go some way toward bridging the distance between what both poetry and religion can reveal to us of the experiences which James called '*ineffable.*' Inspired by the Symbolists, Eliot sought to evoke feelings, moods and experiences by juxtaposing images, e.g. 'Garlic and sapphires' and placing a greater emphasis on a sense of music as accompaniment to these metaphors and symbols, as he urges us toward an apprehension of the 'timeless with time.' The Symbolist adage 'To name is to destroy, to suggest is to create' is applied throughout Four Quartets in an attempt to takes us where the 'Words, after speech, reach into the silence.'

To get to that silence, however, we will need more than an ear for music or an imagination which can unpack symbols; rather we have to take a journey into ourselves – to explore the human condition, the 'twittering world' of Time and the origins of man's propensity for suffering.

CHAPTER 3:
SUFFERING

'The mass of men lead lives of quiet desperation.'
Henry David Thoreau (1817-1862)

Much of T. S. Eliot's poetry is a commentary on the theme of suffering in relation to the human condition. From the self-conscious figure of *The Love Song of J Alfred Prufrock* (1915), whose inner conflicts are revealed in the need to '*prepare a face for the faces you will meet*' to *The Waste Land* (1922), where Eliot gives us the image of crowds of city workers flowing over London Bridge, '*so many, I had not thought death had undone so many.*' Having lived through an era which had witnessed two world wars, Eliot, in the early 1940s, gives us in *Four Quartets* a study of suffering which arguably surpasses that of any of his previous poems.

In the last chapter, we discussed Eliot's

experience in the gardens of *Burnt Norton* and the evocative language which he employs to both recall and share this encounter – the shafts of sunlight filling an empty pool, the invisible presence of a Timeless reality and the echoes of a forgotten ecstasy; with its allusions to Eden. In the third movement of this poem, Eliot takes us far away from the peaceful gardens of *Burnt Norton* and in contrast sits us amid the hustle and bustle of an underground train; a '*place of disaffection*' where the '*strained time-ridden faces*' are:

> '*Distracted from distraction by distraction*
> *Filled with fancies and empty of meaning*
> *Tumid apathy with no concentration*
> *Men and bits of paper...*'

Eliot is said to have taken the image from his daily jaunt between Gloucester Road to Russell Square on the London Underground. The scene is bleak – Eliot calls it a '*twittering world.*'

> '*Time before and time after*
> *Eructation of unhealthy souls*
> *Into the faded air...*'

He uses the same theme again in *East Coker*,

where he talks about the underground train stopping between stations and seeing *'behind every face the mental emptiness'* of those who have nothing to think about.

In these sections of *Burnt Norton* and *East Coker*, Eliot looks beyond the public face of a person's exterior life and exposes us to the fragile inner one. Here the images are of tired and disaffected people – made weary by the routines of their daily lives; wilfully distracted from their feelings of dissatisfaction, powerless before the rotating wheels of time which turn and drive their restless minds.

Elsewhere, this time-bound existence is developed to include, not just the personal experience but also that of our ancestors: *'What was to be the value of the long looked forward to, / Long hoped for calm, the autumnal serenity / And wisdom of age? Had they deceived us / Or deceived themselves, the quiet voiced elders?'*

And further, in The *Dry Salvages*, we come upon the singular voice of humanity in lament:

> *'Where is there an end to it, the soundless wailing*
> *The silent withering of autumn flowers...?*
> *There is no end, but addition: the trailing*
> *Consequence of further days and hours...'*

This is pretty brutal stuff! A direct hit between the eyes: a relentless assault on what is seen as man's banal and meaningless existence. From cradle to grave comes the final sorrow '*to set a crown upon your lifetime's effort*':

'*The cold friction of expiring sense...*
As body and soul begin to fall asunder'

The reward for a lifetime's struggle is an ageing body and a failing mind. In the background a laughter '*which ceases to amuse.*' And then comes the hammer blow: Our suffering was infectious – we passed it on, either in anger or in error, to our lovers, parents, colleagues or brothers: '*...the rending pain of re-enactment / Of all that you have said and done, and been; the shame / Of motives late revealed, and the awareness / Of things ill done and done to others' harm*'

It was important for Eliot to labour this theme of suffering because, of course, it's part of the broader message of his poem: that suffering has a purpose and can be understood and, to a certain extent, transcended. However, what we need to do here is to explore the origins of human suffering, as Eliot understood them. So, let us too take a seat on a metaphorical underground train, as we journey through the traditions of Buddhism and

Christianity in order to develop our understanding of suffering in relation to *Four Quartets*.

Eliot became an Anglo-Catholic in 1927, at the age of 39. However, in his earlier days, he very nearly became a Buddhist – later commenting that he felt himself unable to do so for both practical and sentimental reason. Nevertheless, Buddhism remained an important influence on him throughout his life. And so it's essential that we consider the insights of this religion and its relationship to *Four Quartets*.

The principle teachings of Buddhism are the *Four Holy Truths*. The first, which underpins the whole of Buddhist thought and practice, is neatly packed in the concise statement 'all life is suffering' (dukkha). The Buddha, much like a doctor, diagnosed the human condition and offered a prognosis, that is; he identified suffering as an illness intrinsic to humans and recommended a remedy for its cure – his own teachings (critical thinkers feel free to identify bias). As Buddhism developed it identified three distinct ways in which we suffer: 1. Ordinary suffering. 2. The suffering of change. 3. The suffering of conditioned existence.

Ordinary suffering refers to the process of ageing, illness and death. We can all relate to this one pretty quickly – the cosmetics industry is constantly developing new products to slow down or conceal the effects of ageing, as evidenced by the growing popularity of Botox and cosmetic surgery. Likewise, our dependence on pharmaceuticals (currently estimated to be the world's third richest industry next to oil and one place from the top spot, alcohol) limits our pains and increases the life expectancy of one generation over that of the previous. Death refers predominantly to the grief of separation and loss; the rites of passage for which modern life hardly prepares us for.

You will notice that some of the quotations we have already read from *Four Quartets* fit this category of suffering. Elsewhere in *Four Quartets*, ordinary suffering is referred to as: '*final addition, the failing Pride or resentment of failing powers.*'

More than the dull ache of an arthritic bone, there is the feeling of impotence and shame, as body and mind both embarrass and offend – perhaps a balding head, receding gums or the awkward note of involuntary flatulence. In this ordinary experience of suffering Eliot compares humans to:

'*a drifting boat with a slow leakage.*'

And then, in the graveyard, among ageing headstones – many of which '*cannot be deciphered*' –

stands the yew tree, its fingers *'curled down on us'* as we are taken into death's fold.

The suffering of change in Buddhism refers to distress and anxiety resulting from change in our life situations: from being ignorant of change, not accepting change and change which is beyond our control – change resulting from the ending of happy situations and the changing nature of our personalities, likes and dislikes. We can all think of examples of this suffering in our own lives and the frustration and disappointment which accompany them. Eliot comments in *Dry Salvages*:

'People smile and change, but the agony abides.'

And it's not just we humans – the suffering of change is reflected through our endeavours:

'Houses rise and fall, crumble, are extended,
Are removed, destroyed, restored or in their place
Is an open field, or a factory, or a by pass.'

And finally, the suffering of conditioned existence refers to the dissatisfaction, insecurity or angst which festers in the background of our lives. It's the suffering we might experience from feeling incarcerated by a humdrum existence we feel powerless to change. It is the struggle to find a meaning or a context which enriches and illuminates our everyday human experience. Sometimes referred to as existential suffering, it is the anguish we feel by being enslaved to routines, habits and fears which prevent us from making free choices, from being more actively responsible for our lives and from finding deeper sources of meaning. It is precisely this type of suffering which Eliot focuses on in the underground train and throughout much of his poetry.

Today, we have at our disposal a huge array of technology to keep us stimulated, busied and ultimately distracted from lives which might otherwise seem boring and vacuous. If Eliot were to write *Four Quartets* today, I'm quite sure he would make reference to this technology as a both a symptom of our dissatisfaction and as a vehicle for distraction from it. The *'twittering world'* might become a 'tweeting world'; *'men and bits of paper'* a potential alliteration of 'people, paper, pods and pads'; and *'distraction'* a facebook status update with the mantra 'Distracted from distraction by *7 facts you didn't know about Tom!'* Ok, it doesn't quite have the same poetic impact, but you get my point. We can all, at different levels, relate to this experience of existential emptiness. Today, as our material world becomes an ever greater presence in our lives (not only though technological advances but also advertising, media and fashion) we can each become distracted, overwhelmed and made unwittingly more dependent on the material values which are everywhere marketed as sources of happiness. Of course, science and technology have improved the world around us, but what about the world inside us? Eliot called his own times '*unpropitious*' by which he meant 'without nourishment.' He was talking about war in Europe but he was also talking about the war which takes place inside us, where '*The trilling wire in the blood sings below inveterate scars, appeasing long forgotten wars.*' It was this interior conflict which occupied Eliot through much of his poetry.

The Buddha's concept of suffering as a condition of human experience was inextricably linked to the issue of freewill or personal choice. For Buddhism, it is human thinking, action and restlessness which cause suffering and filter through to suffering. This teaching is echoed in the Eightfold Path, which Buddha taught as a means of release from suffering.

The eight limbs of the path represent the qualities a person should seek to develop in order to overcome their suffering. Divided into three sections, they are: 1. Wisdom: Right View and Right

Intention; 2. Morality: Right Speech, Right Action and Right Livelihood; 3. Meditation: Right Effort; Right Concentration and Right Mindfulness.

In *Four Quartets*, Eliot explicitly states that '*the only wisdom we can hope to acquire is the wisdom of humility,*' which is '*endless.*' Elsewhere, he draws us into thinking about human wisdom indirectly – through its opposite, ignorance. There are Buddhist overtones in much of these lines. He mocks human wisdom as being '*The wisdom only*' of '*dead secrets*' which, imposing a pattern, '*falsifies.*' He vents anger at '*human folly*' then retreats quietly into the '*shame of motives late revealed*' (a reference perhaps to his first wife, Vivienne – whose erratic behaviour led Eliot to separate from her, as she unravelled her way to a mental asylum). Wisdom, as Right View and Right Intention are presented in terms of the human propensity for wrong view and wrong intention:

'*From wrong to wrong the exasperated spirit proceeds*'

Where Eliot talks of '*Tumid apathy with no concentration*' he is referring to a state of laziness so inert that it has become swollen and of a mind which is fickle and restless. These are both characteristics which the Eightfold Path category of Meditation seeks to change through Right Effort and Right

Concentration. Right Action, Speech and Livelihood – aspects of Morality – encourage a spiritual perspective on how to act, speak and work. Quoting *The Bhagavad Gita* – a Hindu text with themes applicable to Buddhism – Eliot says:

> '"*on whatever sphere of being the mind of man may be intent at the time of death*" *that is the one action (and the time of death is every moment) which will fructify in the lives of others.*'

In other words, our attitudes define our actions which, in turn, impact other people. Once the deed is done – be it a harmful physical action, unfavourable words or the questionable business transaction, it – the present action, sets the future in motion. As Eliot said at the poem's beginning:

> '*What might have been and what has been,*
> *Point to one end, which is always present.*'

The Buddha's teachings, summarised in the Eightfold Path, require a person to review his or her attitudes and actions whilst quietening his or her distraction prone mind. Of course, enlightenment won't arrest the processes of ordinary suffering in life but it will free you from unrealistic expectations about the experience of suffering. Likewise, in enlightenment, there will be no cessation of change, only the ending of the individual's attachment to the idea that things are permanent. It will, however, remove any tendency toward feelings that life lacks value or meaning. For Buddhists, the Buddha's path helps people make sense of their lives and what it means to be a human.

We now depart on our metaphorical underground train journey to explore the theme of suffering from our next tradition, Christianity. This journey will be stopping at several stations, ranging in time from the 5th century BCE to the 13th Century CE. On this ride we will meet with ideas from some of the most important religious and spiritual thinkers, including; Epicurus, Irenaeus, Nicholas of Cusa, Julian of Norwich, Augustine and Dante. We will of course, study these figures and their ideas about suffering through the lens of *Four Quartets*.

It should be apparent by now that, whether or not we have a faith position, we each experience suffering in our lives; and more to the point, we each ask the question: why? From the religious perspective of the West, the issue of human suffering is *the* great challenge to faith and the existence of God. The problem was first articulated by the philosopher Epicurus, a non-believer who lived 400 years before Christ. He outlined the accepted qualities of God as all powerful, all knowing, always present and benevolent and, contrasting these with the presence of human suffering, concluded that there could be no such God – for surely – these qualities would require Him to end the suffering (which, being God, he would be perfectly able to do). The alternative, argued Epicurus, is that there is a God but that perhaps He is not all powerful, all knowing, always present or benevolent and that if this is the case, then why even call Him God? Throughout the centuries, religion has had to respond to these arguments, as a matter of personal faith and to save institutional face.

The arguments which seek to defend religion against suffering are called *Theodicies* – from the Greek word 'theo' meaning 'God' and 'dike' meaning 'justice.' One of the earliest theodicies originates from the 2nd century in the person of the Church father – Irenaeus. His defence looks something like this:

1. God allows suffering so that humans can have freewill – who after all wants to be a puppet?

2. The presence of 'evil' is necessary for us to know 'good.'

3. Suffering leads to personal growth and 'soul making.'

4. Although we were created in God's 'image' as the Bible says, we have to grow into his 'likeness' (this may explain the current popularity for beards).

5. Suffering is a test of faith.

The origins of suffering put forward by Irenaeus have several points of interest relevant to our study of Eliot's *Four Quartets*. The Christian concepts of freewill we will save for a discussion further on, along with the idea that suffering is either a test of faith or leads to growth; both of which await us in our next chapter. However, for the moment I would like to focus briefly on second point of Irenaeus' theodicy.

In 'the presence of evil is necessary to know good', we have opposites which are, in a sense, being reconciled; a reconciliation that is, we are told 'necessary.' But why? It's actually a relatively simple idea, but one which has some very important and profound implications. Generally, all abstract ideas or concepts have an opposite. Consider the following – up/down, forward/back, in/out, ugly/ beautiful. An idea or concept cannot exist without reference to its opposite. You simply cannot have the idea of 'perfect' without 'imperfect.' To call something perfect is to, by necessity, make a judgement about something based on its opposite – in this case 'imperfect.' Likewise, something which makes you 'happy' does so because the concept of 'unhappiness' is familiar to you. And so it is that 'good' is known because of 'evil', wrong-doing or bad, whatever your lexicon and therefore has a rightful place in the universe.

The 15th century Christian theologian Nicholas of Cusa developed Irenaeus' idea by coining the Latin phrase *Coincidentia Oppositorum* to explain the oneness of things previously believed to be different. The Latin term *'coincidence of opposites'* means that there is a 'coexistence' between opposites, such as 'good' and 'bad.' They are mutually dependent upon on another. Such insight into the unity of things offers a kind of transcendence; that is, it moves us out of the ordinary perception of things and encourages us to see our reality from a different angle. On a practical everyday level, this 'necessary' reconciliation of opposites enables us to operate at a deeper level of understanding and awareness. If a person experiences suffering through an act which is perceived to be 'bad' the potential power of that suffering to affect a person is diminished if they understand that 'bad' is itself a necessary condition for 'good' to exist. An act of generosity is only an act of generosity because acts of selfishness occur too. This doesn't mean that we sit back with a smile every time we have an experience from which we suffer, but it does mean that these acts will surprise and impact upon us less. On one level, it is about having more realistic expectations of the world in which we live and, on another, it is about understanding that every encounter we have with a negative opposite, for instance – an act of 'cruelty' – is an opportunity to respond with its opposite – 'kindness.' *The New Testament* teaching to 'Love your enemies and do good to those who harm you' is nothing other than a demonstration of this. Hence, by looking at the world from the perspective of opposites we gain both a greater understanding of the reasons for our suffering and a deeper awareness which enables us to cope with it.

For Eliot, this reconciliation of opposites in regard to suffering is most poignantly demonstrated in the line in *Four Quartets* which states:

'Sin is behovely, but
All shall be well, and

All manner of thing shall be well'

'Behove' means 'necessary.' Eliot borrowed the line from the 13th century mystic Julian of Norwich, who said:

'*Sin is behovely, but*
All shall be well, and
All manner of things shall be well.'

It may perhaps seem a little odd for Eliot to be suggesting that sin is necessary. Surely sin is, by default, a bad thing? Doesn't the suggestion that it is necessary run the danger of justifying sinful acts? Well, hopefully some of what I've said above may go some way toward convincing you that, at least on one level, sin has a place in the world purely from the basis of it being the opposite of good. However, before we can discuss further the nature of sin and its relationship to suffering and *Four Quartets*, we need first to address some other, pressing issues, raised by the introduction of the term sin to this discussion.

Sin as an explanation of our suffering is problematic. It's a difficult word and we don't much like it. It belongs to the moralising, guilt pushing, 'do as you're told' dimension of religion which alienates many. As a result, the Christian concept of sin has served to do one of two things for doubting believers and non-believers: it either turns them off religion completely – after which 'religion' as a human activity becomes bracketed in conversation as 'the cause of all wars' or it can turn people to different religions or other forms of spirituality – as evidenced by the growing popularity in recent decades of Eastern religions (perceived to be more practical or philosophical). However, a closer inspection of 'sin' removes some of our confusion and distrust of this word.

Etymologically, the word relates to the idea of 'missing the mark' or 'being off target.' Augustine himself defined sin as *'heart hardening'* – the heart moving away from the Timeless (Spiritual) to Time (material) or vice versa. Earlier in our discussion we talked about centres of value and power. In sin, the centres of value and power become imbalanced or 'off target'. An individual can sway either too much toward the Timeless or to Time.

SIN – POOR SHOOTING?

When the spiritual aspect of a person is pursued at
the cost of the material, a person's sense of humility
can be diminished; a common enough experience
that the Greeks gave it the word *superbia*. In fact,
the Greeks myths are awash with stories warning
of the dangers of superbia. There is the well-known
story of Icarus, who believed he could fly beyond
his human limitations only to come crashing down
to earth. Similarly, the story of the boy Bellerophon
who flew Pegasus to the lofty heights of Mount
Olympus with the intention of overhearing the gods
only to be thrown off the horse. Or the story of

Tantalus, who was punished by the gods for trying to steal their secrets. St. Paul, writing to the community of Christians at Corinth, in the first century, speaks of the dangers of superbia:

'Knowledge puffs up, but love builds up. Anyone who claims to know something does not yet know as they should know.'

Referring to this state of being puffed up through knowledge, Eliot writes in *Four Quartets*:

'...Do not let me hear
Of the wisdom of old men, but rather of their folly...'

'The only wisdom we can hope to acquire
Is the wisdom of humility: humility is endless.'

The opposite presents a problem too – for when the material to be pursued at the cost of the spiritual (which is more often the case), a person tends to develop an overbearing trust or reliance on finite appetites as a source of their stability and happiness; for example – food, entertainment, recognition, status and power.

In *Four Quartets*, Eliot comments that the world moves:

'In appetency, on its metalled ways
Of time past and time future.'

'*Appetency*' refers to the appetites – the insatiable desire or urge for the material or physical sources of value and power.

The 4th century Christian theologian Augustine, later Saint Augustine, went further than Irenaeus in his theodicy by showing that man doesn't just suffer from the freewill of his choice but also the freewill, and subsequent suffering, of Adam and Eve in the garden of Eden (aka original sin). In this story, the tempted Adam and Eve bite into the apple from the tree of knowledge, of which they have been forbidden to eat, and immediately their eyes are opened, whereupon they learnt the difference between good and evil. From this moment, they and all future generations were banished from paradise. Humans had discovered freewill and have been missing the target since. Of course, the story of Adam and Eve is a myth. It is not literally true but works as an allegory for the human condition, suggesting man is born with a capacity to sin and it is sin which leads him away from his natural state of bliss.

In *Dry Salvages*, Eliot refers to Original Sin as a source of human suffering:

'*The bitter apple and the bite in the apple*'

Understanding sin in the ways described above help make it more accessible and acceptable to us. Sin is an imbalance – poor shooting or the outcome of excessive pursuits, either spiritual or material. However you frame it, it is a barrier which prevents humans from experiencing inner peace and happiness. The story of Adam and Eve tells us that humans are born into this state, but there is another story which details this state perhaps more graphically – and its writer had arguably the greatest influence on Eliot's writing. Enter our next Christian thinker – medieval poet, Dante Alighieri.

A Florentine poet, Dante knew a good deal about suffering. He held an unrequited love for Beatrice (who, despite brushing off his affections and dying early in her twenties, remained the love of his life and was later immortalised in his poetry), received death threats and was exiled from his beloved city of Florence. Little wonder he sat down and wrote a book about Hell. The Divine Comedy (the word comedy, refers to the fact that it has a happy ending), is a poem in which Dante, as the character Dante the Pilgrim, journeys through hell, purgatory and paradise, accompanied by his mentor, the 1st century Roman poet, Virgil. Dante, like the Buddha, also spoke symbolically of 'paths', but his path was one from which he had wandered and become lost:

'*Nel mezzo del cammin di nostra vita mi ritrovai per una selva oscura che la diritta via era smarrita*'
'*Midway through the journey of our life I woke to find myself in a dark wood for I had wandered off from the straight path*'

In leaving the path, Dante finds himself at the doorway of Hell – the famous words etched into the rock above the entrance '*Abandon hope all ye who enter here*' prepares us for the grisly sights with which Dante will furnish our imaginations. He and Virgil pass through the vestibule of hell and witness souls damned for refusing to make choices in their lives, of which Dante reports:

'*e dietro le venia si lunga tratta di gente, ch'io non avrei mai creduto, che morte tanta n'avesse disfatta.*'

'and came so long a train of people that I should never have believed death had undone so many.'

You will, no doubt, have noticed that the above quotation was used by Eliot in his earlier poem, *The Waste Land*, to refer to the crowds flowing over London Bridge; as cited at the beginning of this chapter. The image Dante gives us here recalls, in *Four Quartets*, the time strained faces of our disaffected underground train passengers.

Midway through *Four Quartets*, Eliot, halfway through the journey of his own life, reflects: *'So, here I am in the middle way, having had 20 years– / Twenty years largely wasted, the years of l'entre deux guerres–'*

Twenty years wasted, living 'between two wars.' Again, two wars of Europe? Or the wars in Europe and the interior wars of personal suffering?

Advancing through hell, the pilgrim and his mentor hear the wailing laments of the lustful who having subjected their reasoning to carnal desire, are driven on by violent winds; a reflection of the sin for which the souls are punished. Here they meet the lovers Francesca and Paolo, whose infidelity was made famous by Dante. Francesca responds to Dante's inquiry of them:

'*Amor, che a nullo amato amar perdona, mi prese del costui piacer si forte, che come vedi, ancor nom m' abbandona*'

'*Love, which to no loved one permits excuse for loving, took me so strongly with delight in him that, as thou seest, even now it leave me not.*'

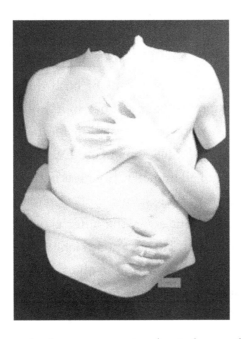

Onwards they venture in the inferno, through successive circles spiralling downwards, each with increased severity, until they reach the centre of the Earth. There, the giant figure of Satan himself resides, frozen in the ice from the waist down; wings flapping like huge sails and three faces each chewing on a victim, one of which is Judas Iscariot. Dante and his mentor climb down through a cavern and find themselves ascending. They have passed through the centre of the Earth and are now going up. A winding path brings them to the surface and to the Island of Mount Purgatory. After a short rest, they begin to climb, passing through seven terraces filled with willing penitents, purging themselves of their sins.

At the exact mid-point of both the poem and the geography of their journey in its entirety, Virgil speaks to Dante on the relationship between love, freewill and sin. He explains to Dante that Love is the source of all human action. It is both natural and elective; the former is our connection to the creator, which is without error, the latter is our freewill to fall in love with His creation. Hence, the soul goes into the world delighting in the products of time. As long as man uses his faculty and gift of reason, (which is what differentiates him from animals) to keep his pleasures in check, and exercises moderation, his soul will not experience suffering. It is only when this love goes unchecked that it can become 'love excessive,' 'love defective' or 'love misguided' (which are what the seven terraces of

Mount Purgatory are divided into) and the soul of man suffers.

Eliot explores this idea in *Burnt Norton*:

'Love is itself unmoving
Only the cause and end of all movement
Timeless, and undesiring
Except in the aspect of time
Caught in the form of limitation'

He reiterates this again, toward the end of *Little Gidding*:

'Who then devised the torment? Love.
Love is the unfamiliar Name
Behind the hands that wove
The intolerable shirt of flame.
We only live, only suspire,
Consumed by either fire or fire.'

Following Dante's teaching, Eliot, in *Four Quartets*, suggests that it is Love which is at the centre of all man's efforts and it is the choice of two loves which defines a person's life.

The seven terraces of Mount Purgatory are divided into the above three categories; on each, one of the seven sins are purged. At the foot of the mountain, a porter etches seven capital Ps onto Dante's forehead, with the tip of his sword. The P stands for Peccato – the Italian word for sin. As Dante passes each terrace a P will be erased. At the foot of the mountain is the most severe – love misguided. Here the sins of Pride, Envy and Anger are purged. Penitents on the terrace of Pride walk with boulders on their backs, to keep them lowly and humble. On the sides of the mountain are carved examples of humility for them to study as they wander the terrace. On the next level is Envy, where the penitent's eye lids are sewn together with iron wire, to teach them the error of looking on their neighbour with jealousy and ill intent; angels call out examples of generosity. On the terrace of Anger, penitents are blinded by thick black smoke which chokes them and which serves to remind them of the sin's disruptive effect on their natural sense. Angels call out prayers of referring to the virtue of meekness.

Dante and Virgil ascend to the terrace of love defective, where they find penitents purging themselves of Sloth. On this terrace the slothful exercise and run – a contrast to the life they led of idleness and indifference. They call out examples of zeal as they run. Within the sins of excessive love we find Greed, Gluttony and Lust. In Greed, or

Covetousness, are the spenders and hoarders – those souls whose ultimate concern in life was material wealth and the power that comes with it. They lay motionless, tied face down into the ground, their eyes fixed upon the earth. The Gluttonous, whose lives were devoted to appeasing the palate and indulging body, are staved in the presence of trees whose fruit is forever out of reach. Fire, a common image for desire, purges the sin of Lust. On this, the 7th and final terrace, we find souls said to be 'refining' themselves in the purgatorial fires.

Commenting on the need for his own 'refining,' Eliot says in *East Coker*:

'If to be warmed, then I must freeze
And quake in frigid purgatorial fires.'

Later, in the second movement of *Little Gidding*, the structure of the lines change as Eliot imitates the Divine Comedy's three line terza rima rhyming style (aba –bcb – cdc) which Dante invented. In this section Eliot meets and wanders the streets with a ghostly figure, a dead master. It is a figure resembling the one Dante himself met in the seventh circle of inferno; his dead teacher, mentor and after his own father's death, guardian – Brunetto Latini. Of this meeting Dante says:

'And I, when he stretched his arm to me, fixed my eyes
on his baked aspect...
I answered, "Are you here, Ser Brunetto?"'

In Eliot's meeting, the figure is described as a
'compound ghost' but certainly he had Dante in
mind:

And as I fixed upon the down-turned face...
I caught the sudden look of a dead master
Whom I had known, forgotten, half recalled
Both one and many; in the brown baked features
The eyes of a familiar compound ghost...'

Eliot's 'dead master' refers to the habitual state of
sin and identifies Love as a fire to purge man of his
suffering:

'From wrong to wrong, the exasperated spirit
Proceeds, unless restored by that refining fire'

Virgil leaves Dante on top of Mount Purgatory
to continue onwards to Paradise, where he is
accompanied by Beatrice on a journey through the
heavenly spheres and onto the empyrean where lies

the source of the love which moves the sun and all the other stars.

Dante's journey through hell and purgatory is an allegory which offers insights into human suffering, or aspects of it. And his poem has as much relevance today as it did when it was written some seven hundred years ago. Our exterior world may have changed but our interior world is largely unchanged.

In Dante's time, the seven capital sins were the result of love excessive, defective or misguided. Today, we might refer to these sins as 'appetites' which both consume and distract us. Dante's 'sin' was a barrier between a person and his or her natural state, which he believed to be love. Again, today, we might call this natural state of love our inner sense of well-being or happiness, which our appetites distort. Overcoming these destructive experiences was then and is now, in essence, what spirituality is all about. It sets us on a path from which we may have strayed and leads us out of the dark wood to a garden where we can find ourselves free among shafts of sunlight.

In this chapter, we have discussed how Eliot perceived suffering in the 'twittering world' of Time and we explored the origins of suffering as he knew them according to Buddhism and Christianity. In Buddhism we discussed the three ways in which a person suffers and linked these to *Four Quartets*. In terms of Christianity, we began with the philosophical challenge of suffering as presented by a non-Christian, Epicurus, and went on to consider how the theodicies of Irenaeus and Augustine offered a defence against the problem of suffering. Our discussion on the *coincidentia oppositorum* of Nicholas of Cusa enabled us to see the necessity of opposites for giving us insight into the unity of things perceived as different. We brought the word 'sin' out of the shadows and were able to see it merely as 'missing the mark' or the imbalanced centres of value and power – the opposite, in fact, of chapter one's intersection of the Timeless and Time. And finally, we explored sin and suffering from Dante's world. Here, we saw that sin is nothing more than a separation from our natural state of Love, which becomes misguided, defective or made excessive through reasoning falling prey to the appetites.

Our discussion on suffering helps us – either directly or indirectly, to better understand Eliot's exploration of this theme in *Four Quartets*. Eliot was heavily influenced by the world views of Buddhism and, of course, Christianity – particularly, Dante. Thus, developing our understanding of these subjects deepens our understanding of Eliot's work.

And it is to the freedom from this suffering we

are now called. What lay ahead of us in the next chapter is the path out of the wood – various paths in fact; and we shall inspect each. Our focus, however, will be on the path Eliot chose.

CHAPTER 4:
FREEDOM

'*Liberta va cercando*'
Virgil speaking of Dante on the foot of Mount
Purgatory I:71

Arriving at the foot of Mount Purgatory, Dante and Virgil are challenged by Cato, guardian to the mountain, who asks – '*Who are ye that have fled the eternal prison... are the laws of the abyss been broken or has a new decree been made in heaven?*' Responding that their journey has been sanctioned by Heaven, Virgil goes onto tell Cato that having passed through hell, his protégé, Dante, goes now in '*search of his freedom.*'

Freedom is the great wealth. For most of us the term wealth refers to money, but money is simply a form of freedom – e.g. it frees us from the stress of making ends meet; it frees us to lock up our homes and take a two week golfing holiday in the Algarve; it might also free us to use private health care. Having time can be another form of freedom. Consider the extent to which a parent values their 'free time.' Physical health too is a form of freedom – that of movement, exercise and sport. And love – which offers us the freedom of friendship and intimacy. Freedom is the real wealth and treasure.

The freedom Dante sought was to be found as he ascended the mountain on his way to Eden, purging sins along the way. His freedom was the freedom from sin – which was the barrier between a person and their natural state, which he believed to be love. In Eliot's poem, this love is the Timeless. And to purge oneself of sin is to realign oneself to the Timeless.

Freedom from sin may seem a million miles away from the more simple freedom a holiday in the Algarve might afford us, but this is not how the mystical journey works. The point of mysticism is to ground the Timeless in Time. The embrace of the everyday mundane realities is part of the completion of the mystic journey. At the end of *East Coker*, Eliot comments:

> *'There is a time for the evening under starlight,*
> *A time for the evening under lamplight*

(The evening with the photograph album)
Love is most nearly itself
When here and now cease to matter.'

To begin to align one's life with the '*intersection of the timeless with time*' does not mean that you float off into a transcendental aura of pure white light wearing lycra and a Superman cape. The normal activities of everyday life continue – an evening spent recalling memories in a photo album or a walk through busy streets, whilst the stars rotate above you.

This 'grounding' or 'return' to the normal everyday activities is highlighted in Plato's famous *Simile of the Cave*. In this story, written in the fifth century BCE, we are presented with the image of a cave full of individuals who, bound to their chairs and facing forward, spend their days watching shadows dance across a wall; which they mistakenly believe to be their only reality. The image, which Plato says is '*drawn from real life*', is comparable with the image Eliot gives us of the individuals in the underground train:

'*...a place of disaffection*
Time before and time after
In a dim light...'

Eliot's underground train can be likened to Plato's cave, insofar as they each represent an individual's total immersion into the temporal world of Time. In both, the Timeless quality of experience is absent – think *Little Gidding* '*not known, because not looked for.*' In Plato's story, however, one of these cave dwellers breaks free from their bindings and, turning round, sees that the shadows are nothing more than puppets suspended in front of a fire. This new knowledge is an illumination which leads to further investigation of all that was previously held to be true. Plato comments that '*having escaped from ignorance*' and seeing the '*empty nonsense*' of their previous condition, the released prisoner would now be '*nearer reality and seeing more correctly.*' In *East Coker*, Eliot refers to this illumination experience as '*a new and shocking valuation of all we have been*' and which leads to a questioning of all that '*was believed in as the most reliable.*'

Leaving the others bound in their seats, Plato's cave dweller discovers the cave exit and ascending upward and out, sees the sun – which was for Plato the symbol of the eternal One. Here the individual experiences the Timeless, the '*source of all that is right and good.*' However, the journey does not stop there. He or she does not, like Icarus, desire to leave the world behind in pursuit of this transcendental experience. Rather, he or she returns to the cave and takes their place amongst the others, the richer for the experience – '*returning again to the prisoners in the cave below, they share their labours and rewards.*' The cave dweller now begins the work of integrating the Timeless vision into his or her everyday experience. Recall Eliot at the end of *Little Gidding*:

> '...the end of all our exploring
> Will be to arrive at the place we first started
> And know the place for the first time.'

In *Four Quartets*, Eliot takes us on a journey through mystical consciousness.

As we shall see this is a spiritual journey which initially sets us apart from the world (the word 'sacred' means: that which is '*set apart*') but which eventually leads us back to the world – where we are free to enjoy, if it pleases us, a game of golf in the Algarve. Throughout the poem Eliot warns us not to stray too far from the world of Time in our pursuit of the Timeless experience. In *Burnt Norton* Eliot gives us the image of the Lotos flower – which bathes its petals in sunlight and is, you will recall, rooted in the mud – suggesting that only with our feet on the ground can we attain the true wisdom. Eliot comments:

*'The only wisdom we can hope to acquire
Is the wisdom of humility: humility is endless.'*

(Interestingly, Dante's ascent up Mount Purgatory begins with the purging of pride; thought to be the worst sin and the opposite of humility, believed to be the highest virtue.)

The cave simile is, as Plato wrote, a *'picture of the enlightenment or ignorance of our human condition.'* A contemporary model of this picture can be found in the writings of Joseph Campbell (d.1987). Campbell, was a noted mythologist and also mentor to Star Wars creator George Lucas (who based his films on Campbell's work). According to Campbell, within the myths he studied, there was a recurring theme which he called the *'monomyth,'* or hero's journey. The title of his most popular book, *The Hero with a Thousand Faces*, conveys this idea. Campbell summarises the hero's journey:

'The hero ventures forth from the world of common day into a region of supernatural wonder: fabulous forces are there encountered and a decisive victory is won: the

hero comes back from this mysterious adventure with the power to bestow boons on his fellow man.'

The hero's journey has three stages – separation, initiation and return. Separation, or what Campbell also refers to as *'the call to adventure,'* involves an awakening or illumination. Initiation involves undergoing a trial; a test or ordeal, whilst return involves bringing back to the community the *'runes of wisdom'* from that trial.

Regarding this return Joseph Campbell comments:

'The first problem of the returning hero is to accept as real, after an experience of the soul-satisfying vision of fulfilment, the passing joys and sorrows, banalities and noisy obscenities of life. Why re-enter such a world? Why attempt to make plausible, or even interesting, to men and women consumed with passion, the experience of transcendental bliss?'

In Platonic terms, the hero, having awoken to the difficult reality of his condition, ascends the cave; where he has a vision of the sun – the Timeless. He experiences an internal conflict in coming to terms with the life he has been living and the life he sees now. Plato comments that *'these actions would be painful... when thinking of his first home and what passed for wisdom there.'*

In trying to make sense of it all, his long established self-wrestles with the newly emerging self. A transformation takes place. He returns to the cave with this new insight and his world is transfigured through it.

Both Plato's Simile of the Cave and Campbell's Hero's Journey correspond to the writings of another important writer, Evelyn Underhill (d.1934). Underhill, writing in her work influential 1911 work *'Mysticism: A Study of the Nature and Development of Man's Spiritual Consciousness'* (a book which Eliot possessed and heavily annotated) identified, like Campbell, various stages through which a person must pass in order to achieve a union of the Timeless with Time. She termed these stages *'Mystic Way.'*

One of the stages in Underhill's mystic way, which more of less aligns with Campbell's 'initiation' stage, is called Dark Night of the Soul – this is not Underhill's term but that of a fifteenth century Christian mystic called St John of the Cross. The Dark Night of the Soul is the stage whereby the individual undergoes what Underhill refers to as a *'mystic death'* – the death of the old self to facilitate the *'remaking of character'* and rebirth of a new self.

Whilst *Four Quartets* awakens us to suffering and

helps us make sense of suffering (as we saw in the previous chapter) it also identifies a way out of suffering. For Eliot, this way out of suffering – out of Dante's dark wood – was through this Dark Night of the Soul; which is also known in mystic circles as the *via negativa* (negative way). To this we must now turn.

The *via negativa* is a mystical pathway of personal transformation, which is discussed by William James in his seminal work *The Varieties of Religious Experience*. We have already discussed James in chapter two, in reference to the ineffability of the mystic experience. Later in the same book, James goes on to describe two types of religious person – the first is described as '*healthy minded*,' and the second, the '*sick soul*.' The latter's experience is synonymous with *The Dark Night of the Soul*. No prizes for guessing under which one of these titles we shall be placing Mr Eliot.

Referring to the healthy minded soul first, James comments that:

'It is hoped that we all have some friend, perhaps more often feminine than masculine, and young than old, whose soul is of this sky blue tint, whose affinities are rather with flowers and birds and all enchanting innocences

than with dark human passions, who can think no ill of man or God...'

You get a sense of where we are going with this – the healthy minded type is essentially a bit of a dreamer. James gives us an example of the healthy minded soul in the person of poet Walt Whitman; whose favourite occupation was, according to one of Whitman's friends *'sauntering outdoors by himself, looking at the grass, the trees and flowers.'* This friend continues: *'He never complained or grumbled either at the weather, pain, illness or anything else. He never swore because he was never angry. He never exhibited fear and I do not believe he felt it.'*

You might consider healthy mindedness a pretty fortunate mind-set. James didn't. He questioned it. He asked whether it was a *'blessed escape'* or a *'fragile fiction.'* He went on to say that:

'To ascribe religious value to mere happy go lucky contentment is nothing other than forgetfulness and superficiality. Let healthy mindedness do its best with its strange power of living in the moment or ignoring and forgetting what is in the background. Yet still the evil background is there – and the skull is grinning at the banquet table.'

An example of Whitman's healthy mindedness can be found in his well-known line, '*Keep your face always toward the sun and the shadows will fall behind you.*' For James, this attitude was pleasant but potentially dangerous. Time is a cave full of shadows. To keep your face always toward the sun is to turn your back on the cave, as though it wasn't there. But it is a fragile happiness which ignores this background. For James the value of the religious experience was not to be found in moments of dreamy contentment but rather in the insight which exposes us to the reality of the human condition. In *Four Quartets*, Eliot suggests that humankind cannot bear very much reality – but he doesn't advocate a running away from our '*twittering world*' of Time but rather, as we shall see, a descent into it; in order that we transform it. As Eliot says '*Only through time is time conquered.*'

The Sick Soul experience is described by James as a rebirth, like Underhill's mystic death. Here the cherished illusions and images of oneself fall away. The Sick Soul consents to being '*stripped down*' as James says, to the barest nothingness in order to be remade. In *Four Quartets*, this process begins at the end of the third movement of *Burnt Norton*, where Eliot asks us to '*descend lower.*' In the previous lines of the same movement we were in an underground train – now we are descending into ourselves; into the darker reaches of self, what Eliot calls 'Internal darkness.' We are alone in our 'perpetual solitude' without the crutch of finite possessions or sensual distractions:

> 'Descend lower, descend only
> Into the world of perpetual solitude,
> World not world, but that which is not world,
> Internal darkness, deprivation
> And destitution of all property
> Desiccation of the world of sense'

In the third movement of *East Coker*, Eliot likens this stripping down and remaking of character to the changes which happen between scenes in the theatre: *'I said to my soul be still, and let the dark come upon you / Which shall be the darkness of God. As in a theatre, / The lights are extinguished, for the scene to be changed / With the hollow humble of wings, with a movement of darkness / On darkness.'*

James was a distinguished scholar who Eliot knew from his Harvard days and it is likely that Eliot borrowed this idea from him; in particular passages where James discusses the case study of a sick soul. This individual commented, of his own religious conversion, that:

'It was as if I was in a theatre; as if people were actors and everything were scenery, always changing.'

This experience of change – or the ending of one particular situation and the beginning of another is known in theological circles as 'eschatology' or 'end time.' In mysticism it is the mystic death – the ending of one life and the beginning of another. Joseph Campbell's famous quote below has eschatological tones:

'We must be willing to get rid of the life we've planned so as to have the life that is waiting for us.'

Understanding eschatology shines a proverbial light on terms like – *'In my beginning is my end.'* Taking the spiritual path might mean the ending of an old life and the beginning of a new one. In the second section of *East Coker*, Eliot gives us all kinds of images as he attempts to describe this internal eschatology or collapsing of self (mystic death). Here the scene is almost, if not actually, apocalyptic. The seasons are disrupted as *'Late roses'* are *'filled with early snow'* the constellations fight, the sun and moon go down and all is:

'Whirled in a vortex that shall bring
The world to that destructive fire
Which burns before the ice-cap reigns'

In this section, Eliot is at the peak of his poetic power – you can almost hear him exhale as he says *'That was a way of putting it – not very satisfactory'.*

Then, in the third movement of *East Coker* we come to the dark night – the *'Dark dark dark. They all go into the dark'* which heralds the coming of St John of the Cross, proper. We have already had an allusion to St John of the Cross at the end of *Burnt Norton*, where Eliot talks of *'... the figure at the ten stairs.'* This is a direct reference to what St John of the Cross calls *'the ten steps of the ladder of love by which the soul ascends to God.'* Ascent on this ladder takes one through – yes, another set of stages of mystical illumination – 'beginner', to 'proficient' and finally ending in 'perfect,' the union of the Timeless with Time. St John of the Cross, like Dante, explains that the ascent to love comes by way of a purging of the seven deadly sins, so that:

'As a sick man loses desire for taste of all food and the colour vanishes from his face, so the soul in this degree of love loses all pleasure in earthly things...'

Eliot begins his paraphrasing of St John of the Cross with a summary of the negative way, the dark night:

'In order to arrive there,
To arrive where you are, to get from where you are not,
You must go by the way wherein there is no ecstasy.'

He then launches into lines which are almost directly lifted from St John of the Cross and laid down in *Four Quartets*; if not for a bit of a polishing first. St John of the Cross says:

'In order to arrive at possessing everything, desire to possess nothing.'

Compare with Eliot:

In order to possess what you do not possess
You must go by the way of dispossession'

Again, St John of the Cross:

'In order to arrive at that point where you know nothing, you must go by a way you do not know.'

Eliot says:

'In order to arrive at what you do not know
You must go by a way which is the way of ignorance.'

William James commented that the *via negative* experience is a *'deeper kind of communion'* which *'opens our eyes to the deepest levels of truth'* (unlike the healthy minded experience of sun gazing). Eliot echoes James at the end of East Coker where he says: *'We must be still and still moving, into another intensity / For a further union, a deeper communion.'*

William James further likened the sick soul's transformation to being *'twice born.'* He summarises the pathway:

'The securest way to peace for the 'twice born' (Sick Soul) is, as a matter of historic fact, through a radical pessimism. More than the observation of nature, life and death, the individual must, in his own person, become prey of melancholy'

Eliot's personal transformation required that he go into the dark; that he become prey to melancholy and that he allow himself to be remade. His mystic death is described in the lines from *East Coker*, which this time carries echoes of Dante:

'The chill ascends from feet to knees
The fever sings in mental wires
If to be warmed then I must freeze
And quake in frigid purgatorial fires.'

In his poem, Ash Wednesday – written shortly
after his conversion to the Anglo-Catholic Church
and before Four Quartets, Eliot refers to St John of
the Cross's ladder of love; which serves to illuminate
further our discussion here. He comments there on
wrestling with the devil as he is remade or in the
process of being twice born:

'At the first turning of the second stair
I turned and saw below
The same shape twisted on the banister
Under the vapour in the fetid air
Struggling with the devil of the stairs who wears
The deceitful face of hope and despair'

And of course, the famous lines of not wanting
to run away from this interior battle or of attaching
oneself to hope:

'Because I do not hope to turn again
Because I do not hope
Because I do not hope to turn'

Part of the experience of the *Dark Night of the Soul* is to abandon all attachments – even those of hope and love. Everything must go in this mystic death. Eliot comments again in Section three of *East Coker*: *'I said to my soul, be still, and wait without hope / For hope would be hope of the wrong thing; wait without love / For love would be love of the wrong thing; there is yet faith / But the faith and the love and the hope are all in the waiting.'*

The mystic death is of course supported and facilitated by Eliot's faith in the Christian revelation – in Christ, the union of spheres. As mentioned previously in Chapter One, Christ is East Coker's *'Wounded surgeon'* who *'plies the steel'* in order to *'question the distempered part'* (the diseased part, that is). One has an image of Eliot laid flat out, etherised upon a surgeon's table being operated on by the 2000 year old Christ.

On the subject of his faith, Eliot comments further that:

'Our only health is the disease
If we obey the dying nurse
Whose constant care is not to please
But to remind of our, and Adam's curse,
And that to be restored, our sickness must grow worse.'

The dying nurse is the Church. St John of the Cross similarly discusses this nursing in *The Dark Night of The Soul*:

'We are to keep in mind that a soul, when seriously converted to the service of God is, in general spiritually nursed and caressed, as an infant by its loving mother,'

In the second movement of *Burnt Norton*, Eliot refers to intersection of the Timeless with Time as: '*The inner freedom from the practical desire, / The release from action and suffering, release from the inner / And the outer compulsion*'

The aim of each of the mystical pathways of personal transformation we have discussed is freedom – freedom from sin and freedom from attachment to the finite (to Time). Whether it is Plato's cave, Campbell's hero, Underhill's mystic death, St John of the Cross's dark night, James' Sick Soul or even Dante's inferno, purgatory and paradise, this freedom brings us in closer relationship to Eliot's '*still point*' or '*intersection*' of the '*timeless with time.*' Eliot's *Four Quartets* relies heavily on these mystic traditions: he reinterprets them, restates them and in some cases rewrites them.

Before paraphrasing St John of the Cross, Eliot comments in *East Coker*:

'You say I am repeating
Something I have said before. I shall say it again?'

Eliot is most definitely saying something both he and others have said before. But then, blowing the dust off a bowl of rose leaves is just part of everyday housekeeping for a poet.

This freedom then tempers both our desires and needs and releases us from our attachments or *'appetency'*. A variety of terms are employed by Eliot to express how this 'release' occurs – 'purging' 'purifying' 'cleansing 'emptying' 'desiccation' 'evacuation' 'burning' 'descent' 'dying' 'dispossession' 'chill' 'desolation' 'deprivation' 'destitution' 'fire' 'freezing' 'detachment' 'discharge' 'renunciation' and 'death'.

However you put it, it all comes down to the one thing – Love. It is love which frames the whole transformation process in *Four Quartets*. Love purges, love redeems and love frees. Love binds us back to our natural state and love illuminates our *'temporal reversions'*. It comes at a cost, however; and the price is everything. As the last section of *Little Gidding* states:

'A condition of compete simplicity
(Costing not less than everything)'

We start out on our journey through *Four
Quartets* by considering our relationship to time, a
necessary but ultimately finite centre of value and
power. In a garden we feel the freedom of another
world, something beyond our normal experience; a
timeless reality. We leave the rural country and take
a tube ride in the city, where we witness our
sufferings through that of others. We question these
feelings of dissatisfaction and we begin to recognise
that we are not free in our finite world at all, but
enchained. We are aware of another level of reality
but find it difficult to describe or explain this
experience, certainly to make sense of it in words;
we know it only in terms of love. This love leads us
to reconsider all that we have been and done and, in
doing this, we begin a journey inside ourselves. We
see fears, appetites and selfishness. In this darkness,
love shines a light on our misguided, defective and
excessive pursuits. We recognise that these
experiences are the barriers to the very thing which
now moves us, as it does the heavens and all the
stars. And we know too that it was the same for
previous generations and all of mankind. Our desire

is now for this other reality and, with the assistance of those who went before us, we begin the process of emptying ourselves of all previously cherished illusions and images, to emerge newly created. Returning to the surface of our world we see everything differently. Love, like a natural medicine clearing the toxins in our body, leaves us humbled and happy, whether the shadow is in front of us or behind.

Little Gidding is the final destination of *Four Quartets*, to which the other three Quartets where always leading. Here, bathed in shafts of sunlight like the lotos flower, we are at Eliot's '*still point.*' Not, of course, in '*time's covenant*' – for we know that Time alone does not redeem, or take us back our natural state. We are in Time and we are out of Time. We are at the intersection, where '*the soul's sap quivers.*'

'*If you came this way*' says Eliot, having left the '*rough road,*' meaning both the single dirt track road that takes you to Little Gidding, as well as the enchainment to finite centres of value and power. '*If you came this way at night fall like a broken king*', meaning both King Charles who visited Little Gidding under the cover of night during the Civil War, as well as the dark night which strips and breaks the self. '*If you came this way,*' continues Eliot '*And turn behind the pig-sty to the dull façade,*' meaning both the house, which was a pig-barn when Eliot visited in 1934, and the simple frontage of St Michael's Church, as well as the unsatisfying reality of living a purely finite experience. *'If you came this way... you would have to put of sense and notion.'* In the presence of the rational and non-rational we are aware of both the physical world around us, which we encounter through sense perception, and a non-physical world, which we encounter through faith and intuition – a trust in something you can't see and can only feel.

'As we grow older, the world becomes stranger', says Eliot. The pattern of living and dying is more complicated than we might first have thought. Perhaps, '...*the time of death is every moment*' as Eliot insists, and that we are free to choose different patterns in our life. He once said he sees *'the path of progress for modern man in his occupation with his own self, with his inner being.'* Reading into what we already know about Eliot from *Four Quartets*, we can be quite sure that he was referring here to the need for a person to pursue and maintain a spiritual perspective in their life and to become *'renewed, transfigured'* by it. Few of us can offer ourselves to a *'lifetime's death in love'* but we can find freedom by embracing our spirituality.

EPILOGUE

In March 2015, I took a short break from completing *Four Quartets – T S Eliot and Spirituality* to take a group of ten students to Florence, Italy. On the final day I made a special effort to visit the Museo Nazionale del Bargello to see Donatello's bronze sculpture – *David*. Just as I was leaving the room I spotted a bronze bust of an individual wearing a large elliptic-shaped medallion on his chest, portraying a winged youth driving a chariot drawn by two horses. I immediately recognised the Platonic allusion. The bust, attributed to Donatello c.1560, was entitled '*Bust of a Neo-Platonist youth.*'

In his work *Phaedrus*, Plato used the metaphor of a chariot pulled by two horses to explain his view of the human soul. He wrote:

'... one of the horses is noble and of noble breed, but the other quite the opposite in breed and character. Therefore in our case the driving is necessarily difficult and troublesome'

Eliot was referring to the same *'difficult and troublesome'* predicament of the soul, in the *Burnt Norton* lines *'Garlic and sapphires in the mud/ Clot the bedded axel-tree.'* An axel-tree is an ancient term for a chariot's chassis. The mud, (from which, you will recall, the lotus flower grows) is a metaphor for Time. 'Garlic and Sapphires', the equivalent of Plato's horses, are the lowly or base and the elevated or noble: the material and spiritual, the Time-bound and Timeless.

Maintaining our chariot involves exercising, nurturing and caring for both the physical and non-physical dimensions of our human experience. This has been the great insight of the sages, philosophers or poets. When these two are balanced and harmonious, then we can find that horizon within ourselves and, as Marsilio Ficino says, 'more widely absorb the one.' And there, in our beginning, is our end.

Acknowledgements

Special thanks to my editing team for labouring through my drafts and offering feedback: Naomi Limer, Oline Eaton, and Andrew Grey.

Permissions:

Four Quartets by T. S. Eliot, 1943

copyright © Faber and Faber Publishing House

Other quotations:

The Hero with a Thousand Faces by Joseph Campbell, copyright © Campbell 1993 by kind permission of Joseph Campbell Foundation (jcf.org)

Reflections on the Art of Living by Joseph Campbell, 1991, copyright © Campbell Copyright 2011 by permission of Joseph Campbell Foundation (jcf.org).

American Beauty by Alan Ball, 1999 (Random House)

Peaks, Values and Human Experience by Abraham Maslow, 1994 (Penguin/Arkana Books)

The Further Reaches of Human Nature by Abraham Maslow, 1993 (Penguin/Arkana Books)

The Symbolist Movement in Literature by Arthur Symons, 2014 (Fyfield Books)

Dynamics of Faith by Paul Tillich, 1957 (HarperOne)

The Republic by Plato, 1987 (Penguin Classics)

Phaedrus by Plato, 1993 (Dover)

The Varieties of Religious Experience by William James, 1985 (Penguin Classics)

The Dark Night of the Soul by St John of the Cross, 1973 (James Clarke)

Picture Acknowledgements

Cover illustration of T. S . Eliot by Stephanie Struth, *tinygremlin.com*

'*All ears*' *Marcushowlett-photography.co.uk*

All other images created by the author.